CHRISTIAN BUSINESS LEADER

The Keys to Thinking Like a Christ Follower in a Corporate Jungle

BY ALEX PENDUCK

TRILOGY
A WHOLLY OWNED SUBSIDIARY OF TBN
PROFESSIONAL PUBLISHING MEETS POWERFUL PROMOTION

The Christian Business Leader

Trilogy Christian Publishers
A Wholly Owned Subsidiary of Trinity Broadcasting Network
2442 Michelle Drive, Tustin, CA 92780

Copyright © 2024 by Alex Penduck

Scripture quotations marked ESV are taken from the ESV® Bible (The Holy Bible, English Standard Version®), copyright © 2001 by Crossway Bibles, a publishing ministry of Good News Publishers. Used by permission. All rights reserved.

Scripture quotations marked NASB are taken from the New American Standard Bible® (NASB), Copyright © 1960, 1962, 1963, 1968, 1971, 1972, 1973, 1975, 1977, 1995 by The Lockman Foundation. Used by permission. www.Lockman.org.

Scripture quotations marked NIV are taken from the Holy Bible, New International Version®, NIV®. Copyright © 1973, 1978, 1984, 2011 by Biblica, Inc.™ Used by permission of Zondervan. All rights reserved worldwide. www.zondervan.com. The "NIV" and "New International Version" are trademarks registered in the United States Patent and Trademark Office by Biblica, Inc.™

Scripture quotations marked NKJV are taken from the New King James Version®. Copyright © 1982 by Thomas Nelson. Used by permission. All rights reserved.

Scripture quotations marked NLT are taken from the Holy Bible, New Living Translation, copyright © 1996, 2004, 2015 by Tyndale House Foundation. Used by permission of Tyndale House Publishers, Inc., Carol Stream, Illinois 60188. All rights reserved.

All rights reserved, including the right to reproduce this book or portions thereof in any form whatsoever. For information, address Trilogy Christian Publishing Rights Department, 2442 Michelle Drive, Tustin, CA 92780.

Trilogy Christian Publishing/ TBN and colophon are trademarks of Trinity Broadcasting Network.

For information about special discounts for bulk purchases, please contact Trilogy Christian Publishing.

Trilogy Disclaimer: The views and content expressed in this book are those of the author and may not necessarily reflect the views and doctrine of Trilogy Christian Publishing or the Trinity Broadcasting Network.

10 9 8 7 6 5 4 3 2 1
Library of Congress Cataloging-in-Publication Data is available.

ISBN 979-8-89041-599-8
ISBN 979-8-89041-600-1 (ebook)

DEDICATION

I DEDICATE THIS BOOK TO MY LATE GRANDFATHER, FREDERICK CLIFFORD Weaver, who showed me it is possible to have a call of God on your life to preach the Gospel of Jesus Christ, yet also to be a successful entrepreneur and businessman without sacrificing the eternal impact you can make for the kingdom of God.

TABLE OF CONTENTS

Dedication iii

Introduction 7
Chapter 1: Starting Again 15
Chapter 2: The Grace Mentality 21
Chapter 3: The Sling Mentality 31
Chapter 4: The Abundance Mentality 41
Chapter 5: The Ambassador Mentality. 51
Chapter 6: The Favored Mentality 59
Chapter 7: The Right Order Mentality 69
Chapter 8: The Manna Mentality 95
Chapter 9: The Present Future Mentality 109
Chapter 10: The Divine Encounter Mentality 123
Chapter 11: The Generous Mentality 131
Chapter 12: The Kingdom Builder Mentality 147
Chapter 13: The Legacy Mentality. 157
Chapter 14: Conclusion 167

About the Author 173

INTRODUCTION

"**Y**OU FEEL STUCK, DON'T YOU?" THAT WAS THE QUESTION MY WIFE posed to me on a hot July afternoon in 2021 as I felt I was in the middle of an emotional and financial breakdown.

Nothing is worse than feeling stuck and having no plan to get out. I was in a type of business and career prison. For the previous twelve years, I had worked for an independent agency in the insurance industry. I had been our agency's number-one producer for the last seven years and had built up what I thought at the time was a good-sized client base and was making good money.

On top of the large commissions I was receiving each month, included in my compensation package was a car allowance, a country club membership, and an aggressive bonus program. The owners of my company really knew what they were doing to make sure I didn't get enticed by the competition. Life was good.

I have been a follower of Jesus Christ for over thirty-six years, a staff pastor for eight years, and a church planter/lead pastor for twelve years (bi-vocational, along with building out my insurance business). I'm no rookie when it comes to faith and a follower of God, but one lesson I keep learning over and over again is that when it feels like life is good, watch out, for a storm may be coming.

Why is that? Can't life just be good all the time? For those who put their trust in the God of Abraham, Isaac, and Jacob, should we have the protection and blessing of God on us at all times? For those who place their trust in Jesus, haven't we already won the victory? Life should be good, right?

At times, life does feel good, but at other times, storms do come, and suddenly, what was calm, peaceful, and tranquil very quickly turns into a man in tears before his wife because he feels stuck and does not know what to do.

Back in 2010, my wife, Raquel, and I felt God had called us to plant a church in our city. We live in Maryland on the East Coast of the United States, in a part of the world where post-modernism quickly turned into a post-Christian culture. We noticed that many of our friends and neighbors were quietly leaving their churches, following a path to "keep up with the Joneses," forsaking their faith, and many ending their marriages. God had placed a burden on our hearts to create a place where this generation would not be lost.

There are many ways to start a church plant: good ways, bad ways, effective ways, and ineffective ways. With little funding and a gung-ho attitude, we launched our church plant doing many things wrong but with a mission to save a generation. Without funding, I had to find myself a job to pay the bills until the church could get up to speed to pay me a salary. That is how I found insurance. I answered a Craigslist ad for an open position at a local insurance agency. Yes, I said that right, "Craigslist." I knew I would leave for the interview and come home with a job, or I would never come home again, for the Craigslist ad was just some murderous scam to take someone out. The good news is that the Craigslist ad was legit.

While it was never my intention to work at that agency for long, I discovered over the course of the next few years that God's plans are certainly not our plans. While our church plant grew little by little, I was also thriving in the marketplace. I started to realize that I could have "God" conversations with people who were far from God at a business networking event as much as I could on a Sunday morning preaching a sermon. In fact, I discovered as God opened some incredible opportunities for me in the business world that maybe God had called me not just to the local church, which I loved so much, but also to the marketplace.

Never underestimate the grace God has on your life or the environments He will place you in. Understanding what God is doing in the present is just as, if not more important, than understanding where God is taking you in the future. If God is blessing you in one setting, very often, He is blessing you in order to be a blessing to others.

I began to love my bi-vocational role. My joy in being able to give generously to our church instead of having to "take" a salary from our church was immense. I loved to be able to teach about money because I never felt the burden that these people were "paying my salary." It's funny to look back on now because I had such a wrong mentality about the negativity of a pastor taking a salary from the church. Listen, churches should be paying their pastors and paying them well. This is what I found out from twelve years of being a bi-vocational pastor: a bad day as a pastor is a bad day! It can affect their mind, body, spirit, and soul for weeks. A bad day in business, yes, is a bad day, but it pales in comparison to your pastor's bad day. The stress of being a pastor is so much more than the stress I have ever felt in business. This is why we need to pay our pastors well; they deserve it!

Toward the end of 2019, I felt my time leading our church as their lead pastor had come to an end. I thought they needed a new vision and a new voice. In early 2020, after much prayer and guidance, I announced to our leadership team the decision to step down. The plan was that my associate pastor would step into the role of lead pastor, then for our family to go on a three-month sabbatical, and then come back and help with the transition. Aren't plans great? Yes, until storms get in the way.

The first storm to happen was the big "C" storm: Covid! The world shutting down is not a great situation for a leadership change. The transition got delayed, we never went on sabbatical, and long story short, in July of 2020, I passed on the leadership of our church, and we stepped away. It was a hard, gut-wrenching season, not because we were transitioning out, we knew God had led us to this decision, but because of Covid restrictions, we could not look people in the eye whom we had led for so many years, give them a hug and tell them we love them and still believe in them. It was hard, but then again, leadership is complex, and not everything turns out as you plan.

For the next year, apart from trying not to get Covid and preparing for the end of the world, my only focus was on my insurance business. While many lost their jobs and suffered economic hardships, I actually doubled down. With my extra time, I focused on taking better care of my clients and ended 2020 with a record year in sales.

What I did not see at the time, while I was so focused on my job, is that the world, our culture, and its values were changing faster than they ever had in such a short space of time. The world was getting divided over lockdowns, vaccines, masks, political and racial issues, even toilet paper was in short supply, and people were fighting in the grocery stores so much that many of us settled for one-ply sandpaper toilet paper over our regular Charmin Ultra Soft! Our grandchildren in years to come will never believe us when we tell them we had to use one-ply paper!

As the world changed, so did the culture and values in many workplaces. What followed was what became known as the great resignation across corporate America, where many were quitting their jobs and moving on in record numbers. I noticed this shift in our company, and when asked to do several things that I knew violated my own and my family's values in order to lead the way and be an example to the other employees, I knew my time was coming to an end.

This led me to that hot July afternoon when my wife asked me, "You feel stuck, don't you?" My reply was yes! The industry I was in paid you in commissions. Insurance sales is a little different from most other higher-caliber sales jobs. The commission you receive on a sale is decent, but very few are getting rich on a one-time sale. The secret sauce with insurance is what is known as a residual commission. You make a commission on the first year's sale, but if you can keep that client on the books the next year when their renewal comes around, you get paid the same commission percentage again. So if you only made ten sales a year but were able to keep your clients for, say, five years, and, let's say the commission of each sale is $5,000, this is what one to five years would look like in commissions:

YEAR	# OF SALES	TOTAL REVENUE
Year 1	10 sales	$50,000
Year 2	10 sales + 10 renewals	$100,000
Year 3	10 sales + 20 renewals	$150,000
Year 4	10 sales + 30 renewals	$200,000
Year 5	10 sales + 40 renewals	$250,000

Now, this is not a perfect world, and the reality is that you will not keep 100 percent of your clients each year. Furthermore, you must split commissions with owners, support staff, expenses, technology, etc. However, I hope by now you get the concept. In insurance, you don't get rich the first year, but the longer you are in it, the more lucrative it becomes, and many insurance agents retire very wealthy.

There is one problem, though, like the majority of higher-caliber sales jobs: non-competes/non-solicitations. It is commonplace for companies to make their employees sign a contract that states that if they resign from the company or are fired, they cannot take their clients with them for a certain period. Likewise, many contracts state that those said employees cannot even work in the same role for another company in a said geographical location for a certain period of time. The whole point of these contracts is to protect the business from someone leaving and taking all their clients. I get it; I'm not opposed to these contracts; in fact, I believe that, in many cases, they are needed. However, when you are on the other side of these contracts, it can make you feel stuck!

The reality for me on that July afternoon was that I knew for the sake of my faith, my family, and my values, I had to leave the company I had seen so much success for over the last twelve years, but it meant leaving my large book of business which was my income due to my non-solicit agreement. How could we survive? I had already scouted the market, and while I had several job offers with good compensation agreements, no one in insurance could offer me the money I was currently making if I could not bring my clients over with me. It just didn't make economic sense to them. Talk about golden handcuffs. I was well and truly stuck!

This is the place I want to start, as it was out of that season of my life that I discovered what it truly means to be a Christian business leader. While many of the concepts I am going to discuss I have already practiced for many years, some of them have been learned through a season of trusting and looking to God. I'm looking forward to sharing these with you in the hope that one and even maybe all of them can not only enhance your personal life but also help enhance and expand the kingdom of God in the environments you find yourself in.

These concepts, which I call mentalities, are not micro strategies to help you grow a successful business; they are what I believe are God-inspired, Holy Spirit-led mindset shifts to help you build an effective life that will maximize its effectiveness for the kingdom of God. Many of these thoughts are in direct comparison to how the world around you will teach you how to succeed. I do not know about you, but I would rather take my chance on doing this journey we call life God's way instead of the world's way.

CHAPTER 1:
Starting Again

HAVE YOU EVER BUILT SOMETHING BUT REALIZED AS YOU WERE building that you had missed a piece along the way? I have done this many times with self-assembly furniture that I have purchased. As my wisdom has grown throughout the decades, I have discovered that it is better to pick up the assembly guide than it is trying to figure it out on your own. However, even still, the number of times I have misread the manual or gone too fast and discovered a few steps along the way that I attached one section back to front, and now I have to disassemble what I have built so I can rebuild it correctly.

The biggest issue for many of us is that we want to enjoy the finished product quickly and do not enjoy the process of putting the product together. You did not buy that table or dresser from Ikea because you get a kick out of furniture assembly; you bought it to enjoy the finished product. The same is often true for those of us in the business world. You did not pour all that time into your schooling, those early morning networking events, that product development, those seasons of mind-numbing cold calling, or those endless meetings trying to create effective systems because you enjoy those processes (and if you do, then you probably should create a business around them because you are either crazy or gifted!), you did them because you understand that out of these tasks and seasons of immense hard work comes a product or a lifestyle that you can enjoy and do the things you want to do.

As we grow in our faith and wisdom, it is easy to look back and see all those steps we got wrong. The times when we went too fast and didn't read the owner's manual correctly, or those times when we put off the challenging tasks ahead of us for too long that we missed the opportunities in front of us that could have accelerated our goals. Experience and self-discovery are wonderful gifts if you are willing to use them. Do not be surprised in business or life when God allows a storm to jolt you from head to foot, a tidal wave that stops you in your tracks and may even cause you to take a few steps back! Not because God wants to stop your progress, but because God knows that we are prone to making mistakes, often trying to build a life without correctly reading the manual (or sometimes reading the wrong manual). He does not want us to go too far along without correcting the mistake. The storm is there to help us identify and correct the error.

Out of that question, my wife asked me on that hot July afternoon, "You feel stuck, don't you?" A journey began that I will forever be grateful to God for. It has been one of the most arduous journeys I have ever embarked on, a journey of deep self-evaluation, great faith, and discovery. It has been a journey that very few people in my life even knew I was undertaking, but a journey that has forever changed me and marked me.

Throughout the following chapters, I have laid a framework for how God changed me through this journey. While the result has been a change in many of the physical and tangible aspects of my life, the real change has been within my mentality. We hear a lot today about our mindset. From motivational speakers to coaches to pastors to self-help gurus, mindset is a hot topic. I do agree with much that is said about mindset. A clear, cohesive, confident mind gives you the platform to do great and marvelous things. Often, it is a wrong mindset that stops people from succeeding, not their gifts, abilities, or opportunities. However, this is not a self-help book but a God-help book. In truth, it is going to be very hard to put into practice any of the mindset shifts I propose by doing it on your own. In fact, if you are looking to help yourself, then this book is not for you, and you will find very little use in it; you would be better off going to the self-help section of your local library and reading those books instead.

The practices and mind-shifts we will journey on in the following chapters can be taught to others but can only be fully embraced out of a deep faith in our Heavenly Father. While these truths are for the business leader, they do not come from an MBA textbook or out of a corporate boardroom. They have come out of the Bible. When I put what I believe are Godly truths into practice, I have walked through my greatest successes without striving and hustling as much as others.

The reality is that I sometimes feel I am cheating the system. I see others working long, hard hours doing what the experts tell them to get ahead at sometimes significant cost to their families and values. The Jesus way is different! Don't get me wrong, there is no room for laziness; you have to work hard, but when you decide to God-help your life instead of self-help your life, the journey not only becomes "easy" (we will discuss "easy" shortly), but it becomes enjoyable, counter-cultural, faith-filled with enough time and energy to smell the roses along the way.

In the remaining chapters, I talk about a mentality change that needs to occur not only in our minds but a change that needs to transcend in our hearts. The apostle Paul wrote about this to the Roman church when he said:

> *Therefore, I urge you, brothers and sisters, in view of God's mercy, to offer your bodies as a living sacrifice, holy and pleasing to God—this is your true and proper worship. Do not conform to the pattern of this world, but be transformed by the renewing of your mind. Then you will be able to test and approve what God's will is—his good, pleasing, and perfect will.*
>
> — Romans 12:1–2 (NIV)

Worship to God starts with offering yourself to God. One of the ways to worship God is to offer a holy life to God. Holy means "set apart." To be different, not like the rest. Paul commands the Romans not to follow the patterns of this world but to let their minds be transformed or renewed. It is out of a transformed mind, a mind renewed by God that transcends to a changed heart, that we discover God's perfect, pleasing will for our lives.

The world around us, especially the business world, has a pattern of success. They promise big homes, expensive cars, and a life of luxury if you follow them. This pattern has resulted in many wealthy people, but at what cost? It is a pattern that has resulted in many becoming successful, but that has caused even more to hit rock bottom. You see, the pattern of this world is all built on you! I do not know about you, but the older I get, the more successes and failures I face, the more I understand

I'm not strong enough, talented enough, or smart enough to bank my future on me, and I am going to fail!

This is why I need God-help, not self-help. If I follow a pattern, a model, a process, I am going to do it with certainty, and the only certainty in the world we live in is God and God alone! Isaiah 55 tells us that God's ways and thoughts are not the same as ours. His ways are so much higher and more significant. Man-made success is excellent for a season, but God-made success is world-changing. If you want God-made success, it starts by not copying the pattern of the world around you. It begins by letting God change your mentality and transforming the way you think.

CHAPTER 2:

The Grace Mentality

IF YOU WANT TO BE GREAT, YOU HAVE TO WORK HARD! IF YOU WANT TO be successful, you have to put in the hard time. If you want to be the best, then you have to practice hard when no one else is around. If you want to exceed those goals, you have to do the hard grind. If you want to be a successful entrepreneur, then you have to hustle and hustle hard. If you wish to become VP or partner, you have to show others you can do the hard jobs.

I could not agree more with each of these statements. The most successful people are not the lazy ones who coasted their way to the top. If you ask the top entrepreneurs, the best CEOs, the most decorated athletes, the award-winning scientists, and the top 5 percent of sales professionals, they will all tell you that they worked their socks off to get where they were; it was not by chance.

I have been trying to teach my son that talent alone will not get him to the Premier League. He is a soccer fanatic, and all he wants to do is become the next Lionel Messi. However, he has a problem; he just thinks if he is passionate enough about soccer, learns tricks, and plays enough, he will make it. This is a lesson he is learning early in his life: to make it to the top, you have to learn, practice, and execute drills, patterns, and theory, as well as get into the best mental and physical conditioning, even when it hurts. When all his friends have gone inside and are enjoying ice cream, he has to keep working. He can go get the ice cream with his friends, but if he really wants to make it to the Premier League, then what is required is more hard work.

This hard work mentality is hard to argue. The results speak for themselves. You constantly hear it and see it from the self-help gurus and the top business leaders; no one gets anywhere for an extended period of time without hard work!

There is an issue, though: why is it always *hard* work? From the beginning of humanity, we see a fall from perfection. Adam and Eve live in the Garden of Eden in a perfect world that would be even harder for Hollywood to imagine. Life is easy! Adam has been given two jobs; the first one was a project, which was to name all the animals. Using his inventive, creative skills, you could imagine his mental juices following as he got on a roll and named the lion, the bear, the elephant, the panther, the ant, and the dog. He probably had drunk a little too much juice from those grapes when he named the hippopotamus or had a bad pizza the night before when he named the chicken turtle! However, what to many would have seemed like a daunting and overwhelming task was easy for Adam.

The second job, which became his regular job, was to care for and cultivate the Garden of Eden as well. To make sure it did not overgrow, to harvest food from it, and to keep it beautiful. Again, this was easy for Adam. There were no Monday morning blues, no coming home late at night not wanting Eve to even mention work, and no stressed-out weekends or loss of sleep. It was perfect. It was perfect because we were created to work. We were not created to sit around and achieve nothing; no, we were created in the image and likeness of God. Therefore, just like God works, so should we. As God creates, we were created to be creative. As God cultivates, so we should cultivate. Without work, humanity quickly loses perspective and purpose.

When God created Adam, there was no micro-managing from God. Adam was given the freedom to work as he pleased with one restriction: not to eat from a tree called "The Tree of the Knowledge of Good and Evil." There were boundaries in place. God was a good boss. He appointed Adam to work on his strengths. God gave him a rewarding job, paid him well (Adam had free reign to eat almost anything from the Garden), and was clear in His expectations of Adam. Can you imagine living in a perfect world, with a perfect boss, with a perfect family, with complete clarity of mind, body, and soul? No, I can't imagine it either!

Up until Adam and Eve had their famous fall from perfection when the serpent deceived them into eating the forbidden fruit of the Tree of Knowledge of Good and Evil, their life and work were easy. Notice the distinction between how Adam functioned in the Garden and how some of the top people in business, politics, sports, and science are today. For Adam, the way to the top was easy; for corporate America, it is hard.

We cannot miss this important distinction because when Adam falls into sin, there is a consequence. God tells the cost of Adam's sin in Genesis 3.

> *To Adam, He (God) said, "Because you listened to your wife and ate fruit from the tree about which I*

commanded you, 'You must not eat from it,' "*Cursed is the ground because of you; through painful toil you will eat food from it all the days of your life. It will produce thorns and thistles for you, and you will eat the plants of the field. By the sweat of your brow you will eat your food until you return to the ground, since from it you were taken; for dust you are and to dust you will return.*"

— Genesis 3:17–19 (NIV)

Did you catch what God said to Adam? "By the sweat of your brow you will eat" (Genesis 17:19, NIV). To sweat from working hard is a consequence of sin! We live in a world where people boast about their hard work. They boast about their sweat. They tell others in confidence how they had to hustle and put in the sweat equity. However, sweat equity is a result of sin! Think about this for a moment. Before the fall, Adam was successful, but he didn't sweat. After the fall, he was unsuccessful, for those thorns and thistles took the place of the ripe vines of grapes, yet he sweated. Just a few moments of pulling weeds in your yard should tell you everything you need to know about the consequences of sin; sweating from work is not fun.

Jesus was a radical because He was counter-cultural. He lived and taught in a way that shifted people's belief system from what they always believed to a newer, better belief system. The ultimate goal of Jesus, as the book of Hebrews puts it, was to become a second Adam, a better Adam, one that would not fall into sin but one that would come and deliver God's people out of sin. Jesus did this when He lived a sinless life, died as an atoning lamb on a wooden cross, and was resurrected from the dead three days later. In the moment that He died, Jesus broke the curse of sin!

What was the curse of sin? Firstly, it was death, but it was also sweat! Now, I'm not saying that if we believe in Jesus and allow Him to change us from the inside out, our sweatpours are never going to open. Just go outside on a hot, humid July day in Florida, and you will realize that we sweat and some people should never wear colored shirts, for they sweat a whole lot more than other people! What I am saying is if Jesus broke the curse, then why do we think the only way to the top is through hustle and sweat equity? I am not saying that we should not work; we should work. We were created to work. To honor God, we should work with excellence and dignity and give our all, but why do we think it needs to be hard?

Jesus made an incredible statement in Matthew 11 that even through all the years I have taught the Bible, I still do not believe I have fully grasped the magnitude of that statement. He said, "Come to me, all of you who are weary and carry heavy burdens, and I will give you rest. Take my yoke upon you. Let me teach you, because I am humble and gentle at heart, and you will find rest for our souls. For my yoke is easy to bear, and the burden I give you is light" (Matthew 11:28–30, NLT).

Just look at the contrast between Adam's consequence and Jesus' promise. The consequence results in sweat and pain; the promise is a light burden and rest. Jesus is saying, "Look, I know you all believe the way to a successful life is by working hard till you cannot work anymore, but I want to show you a different way, a way to be even more successful without the consequences that Adam suffered."

This is why I call the first mindset that, as Christian business leaders, we must embrace the grace mentality. The word "grace" means undeserved kindness and favor. We are blessed not because we deserve it but because of the kindness of the one who gives it. If you had a newborn baby come into your office, I guarantee you would stop what you are doing and show kindness to that baby. There is no other productivity killer in the offices of America like a baby or a puppy who pays a visit. If they appear, you can forget about your staff doing any work for the next hour or so. You do not give the baby kindness because they have worked for it; no, you give the baby kindness because they are a joy.

This is actually how God sees you. When God thinks about you, He is not thinking about how much you hustled and put in that sweat equity; no, when God thinks about you, He pours out His grace (undeserved kindness) on you because you bring Him joy! He gave up His life and died for you because you are His joy! His love is not conditioned on how hard you work; His love is unconditional.

Our culture loves to highlight the "self-made" man. In truth, there is no such thing. Every successful person has others to thank; there is not anyone who got there all by themselves. We cannot help ourselves, though. The award ceremonies, the circles of excellence trips, the designations, we love them, not because they are good for our soul (well, maybe a President's Club trip to a Caribbean island is), but because they prove how hard we worked and others can see it too.

Now, to be honest, you are not as great as you think you are! Yes, you may have some success, but what was the cost? Was it ultimately worth it? Was it really all because of you? Was it just down to the amount of sweat equity you put it? If you are to be honest, I bet you often doubt yourself. You may, at times, feel like a fraud if people really knew how you felt. The burden of success or trying to be successful has become too heavy; you wish you didn't have to give up so much to get where you believe you need to be. If that is you, then there is hope. There is a better way. It is time to learn the grace mentality.

When Jesus told His listeners that His yoke was easy and His burden was light, it was not because living a life following Christ is easy; in fact, it is quite the opposite. Living the life Jesus desires you to live is actually incredibly difficult. It is counter-cultural, a life of sacrificing what feels good for the sake of what is best. There is a reason that so many do not follow Jesus. It is not because they do not believe in God; it's because of the cost. The cost is great, but the cost to follow the world's way is even greater.

There is a cost to the world's way and a cost to living the Jesus way, but you have to choose your cost. The world's cost is hard work, hustle, and sweat. Jesus' way is giving up! Yes, you heard me right, giving up. It is about giving up your life, often your dreams, ambitions, and desires, and replacing them with His dreams and desires for your life. It is a giving up to the world mindset and replacing it with the grace mindset.

So, what is the grace mentality? It is very simple: it is the understanding that I am not here today because of me. My success, my lifestyle, my career, my awards, and my accolades are not because of me; they are always because of Christ and Christ alone. It is nothing that I have done; it is all because of what Jesus has done. Yes, but what about that all-nighter I pulled to land that big account? What about that business that I turned around? What about that team I led that had record production? The project that no one thought was possible, and I got it done? Yes, good for you, but it's still nothing you have done. It is all because of Christ. The moment you start to look to yourself instead of to Jesus is the moment to begin to choose the world's cost and ignore the cost of living for Jesus.

It is a mindset shift, especially for those who have tasted success. I remember many years back when I started to exceed the sales goals I had been given. People began to view me differently; instead of being another body in the room, I started to get respect, and respect turned into a lot of questions asked toward me. What is the secret of your success? What did you do to build your book of business? What advice can you give someone starting out? I will be honest: I hated those questions because I did not have an answer at the time. I did not feel successful even though I had been. I didn't have a playbook like so many of those famous businessmen who sell their programs to the masses. All I could say was, "It's just the grace of God; I'm nothing special." That was correct; it was the grace of God. It certainly was not because of my head smarts or my cold-calling technique. If it had been left to that, I would have been homeless without a job. What I did not understand at the time was that living in grace is not just realizing I'm not that good; it is understanding that by giving up, you are opening up room for Jesus to work, and when Jesus works, the world around you comes to life!

In those early years, there was a grace on my life. I didn't seem to sweat and hustle like the others in my industry, yet

I still got ahead. I didn't stress and panic like my peers, even though there were many incredibly stressful moments. When you walk in step with Jesus, He starts to lift the burden, not to remove it, but to carry it. Having a grace on your life means you will walk into places, win accounts, meet people, and develop systems you did not deserve, but because of the kindness and favor of God, you will receive what you did not earn nonetheless. Why? Because you are His joy, and He wants to show His kindness to you.

When you walk in the grace of God, the favor on your life accelerates. We will talk about this in a later chapter, but it is crucial never to forget that grace always results in favor, and favor is always the result of grace.

When you walk in the grace of God, the blessings on your life are accelerated. These blessings are both for you to enjoy and also for you to bless others. Always remember, we are blessed to be a blessing. Never get into a habit of eating all your blessings. A blessing sowed into others will reap blessings for them as well. Your purpose is to leave a legacy for others to walk in.

When you walk in the grace of God, the influence on your life accelerates. This grace differs from the life of your partners, co-workers, clients, and competitors. Different always attracts. Sometimes differences bring good attraction, and sometimes they bring bad attraction, but the grace of God will cause others to see you, and when they see you, then influence follows.

When you walk in the grace of God, you have an undeniable mentality that this is all because of Christ, not because of me! The reward for this mentality is that you will start to have to hustle and sweat less as you allow Jesus to come alongside you, take the weight, and give you rest.

Are you ready to let God change the way you think? It does not have to be as hard as what the world says. Let Jesus carry the weight for you as you allow His grace to abound in your life.

PRAYER FOR GRACE

Father, help me to understand that I am nothing without you. All that I have is because of you and because of your incredible grace and love. Help me to acknowledge my depravity without you and give me the awareness to understand what you have truly done for me. Grant me the awareness to show others the grace that you have given me and work in myself so that I do not get prideful when blessings come, for I know that everything I have is all because of Jesus and what He has done for me. Thank you, God, for the grace upon my life that you have poured out in love.

CHAPTER 3:

The Sling Mentality

SALES IS A NUMBERS GAME! THAT IS WHAT ALL THE EXPERTS HAVE preached over the years. In my years of sales, I have come to believe that this is the dominant philosophy when it comes to being successful in that field. I have witnessed it play out, and yes, the majority of the time, the numbers reflect who will be successful and who will not.

The numbers game is pretty simple. The more calls you make to prospects, the more meetings you will get. The more meetings you get, the more opportunities you get to propose your product, and the more proposals you give, the more sales you will make. The numbers game requires much work, but it has been proven over and over again. In sales, there is a term for this game: the pipeline. Imagine an orange press. The idea of an orange press is to get orange juice, but first, before you can get any orange juice, you have to gather some oranges. Then you have to cut the oranges. After cutting the oranges, you put them in the press; after they are squeezed, orange juice drips out. If you have one of those automatic machines that does all the pressing for you, then it's pretty easy to make orange juice, but if you have a manual press, you will quickly find out that it is a lot of work for little juice. This is the sales pipeline; think of prospects and cold calls like oranges. The more you put into the pipeline, the law of numbers will eventually work in your favor, and you will get the juice, the sale!

Pick up any sales book, and they will, in some roundabout way, talk about this numbers game. I believed it and even told people to lean into it who are either new or struggling in sales. The question is usually, "I'm struggling to meet my goal. I work hard and have a great product; why am I not making enough sales?" To which I answer, "What is your close ratio? To figure out your close ratio, you calculate how many proposals, on average, you have to make before you make a sale; that is your close ratio. Once you know how many proposals you need to make, then figure out how many meetings you need before you get a green light to make a proposal, and once you figure that out, do the same for the number of calls you need to make to get a meeting. Once you know your numbers, start making that number of calls to prospects. It will solve your issue of not making enough sales; you have a pipeline issue, fix the pipeline, and you will meet your sales goals."

While this book is not a sales professional book, this type of philosophy is essential to understand, for I believe the same type of mentality is everywhere, whatever type of field or industry you are in.

Chris came to work for our company as a sales executive after a successful career in the sports branding industry. He had decided to leave what he called "corporate America" in order to gain more control over this compensation and time. Chris was a hard worker and very professional; he listened and implemented all the sales training he received. He listened to his mentors and implemented the methods they had used to make them successful in sales. The only issue for Chris was it didn't work. There was an issue with the numbers game that left the experts scratching their heads. Many would say his messaging when he was making calls was weak; others would say his upfront research was lacking good resources. Some said his closing technique lacked the skill to close deals, while he blamed a tough economy and market.

One day, I sat down in Chris' office to check in on him, and he looked plain worn out. We talked through what he was doing, and I tried to coach him through his difficult day. He had come to the revelation that in order to make some good sales, it was going to take work and a lot of hard work. It was in his office that day that I had this thought to myself: *There has to be a better way!* I thought about my own sales pipeline; I did not work as hard as Chris, I had not implemented the sales techniques all the experts taught as Chris did, and I had done the opposite of what many of my mentors had told me to do, yet my sales were off the charts, and his were almost non-existent. It was there in his office that I suddenly remembered David, the King of Israel, and discovered the sling mentality.

The grace mentality we learned of in the previous chapter leads us to Jesus. He takes the heavy lifting so we can rest easily. We were created to work and to have a good work ethic, but it was sin that caused us to sweat while we worked. Chris was sweating that day when I walked into his office. I believe when Jesus said to come to me all who are weary and carry heavy burdens, He was not just talking to those who had lived under a religious theology of working your way to God like the

Jewish people of Jesus' day were. I believe He was talking holistically to all of us in every aspect of our life. He was talking to the Jewish listeners who believed the only way to appease God was to do all the religious duties assigned, but He was also talking to Chris, the sales executive trying to make a sale. There is an easier way.

In 1 Samuel 17, we see one of the most well-known stories in the Bible. The Israelites are at war with the Philistines, their fiercest enemies. It was a war that seemed to be unending, a real back and forth. Without question, Israel was working hard to keep their freedom and to become victorious. This is when the Philistines bring out their champion, a giant from Gath called Goliath. Goliath came with a challenge, a one-on-one, man-on-man combat challenge. Israel was invited to send out their best warrior to individually fight Goliath. The winner of this street fight would see their nation victorious in battle, and the loser would cause their nation to surrender to the other nation. The odds usually would have been fifty-fifty until the Israelites took a look at Goliath. Many biblical commentators believe Goliath was as tall as 9 feet 2–9 inches. I don't think the 2–9 inches really matter; the man was over *nine* feet tall! The armies of Israel froze with fear.

This is where David comes into the picture. Long before he became King David, even before he became one of the most successful warriors in Israel's history, while he was still a shepherd boy, doing an errand for his father delivering food to his brothers who were in Israel's army, David shows us a shift in mentality to how those who put their trust in God approach giants versus how the world approach giants.

Not one man stepped forward from the camp of Israel to fight Goliath. These men had trained for war; they had the resources and the experience to fight. Clothed in armor and swords, they were equipped, but no one volunteered; fear gripped the camp. Israel had trained their men to fight people on their own level, but there weren't any giants in Israel to train against. How were these men, even their strongest, most skilled fighters, to go up against the giant champion from Gath?

When David heard the taunts of the Philistine giant, something set off within him. It was either the blind innocence of youth or something greater within him that welled up to the point that he went to see the Israelite King, Saul, in a request to take on the giant himself. Goliath taunted Israel, poked fun at their God, and ultimately stood in front of the Israelites, representing the world's system, which is that the strongest wins.

When you are so connected to the world's system of success, do not be surprised when you freeze in fear if confronted by the giants the world has never seen before. The year 2020 was a perfect example of a world that froze in fear at a disease that was uncontrollable. Governments and health authorities did not know what to do; there was panic everywhere. However, David, the Shepherd boy from Bethlehem, was not connected to the way the world thinks. He was not trained or experienced as the Israelite army was. David had a different experience. David knew there was another way, God's way!

When King Saul questions David's sanity for wanting to fight the giant, David explains that he has experience; it is just a different kind of experience. As a shepherd, he had killed bears and lions to protect his sheep, and in the same way, he would take down what he called this "uncircumcised Philistine." While the rest of Israel viewed Goliath as their superior competition to defeat, David viewed Goliath as a predator who wanted to destroy God's sheep. While Goliath did not change, he was still an imposing giant figure; David's mentality had changed. For David, this was as much a spiritual war as it was a physical war.

Your business, your career, your workplace, that boardroom, those meetings, believe it or not, but they are as spiritual as they are physical. So often, we go into a church service thinking in the spiritual, but we go into the boardroom or a client meeting thinking in the physical. When God is with you, He is not just with you in the church service. He is with you in the office, on the factory floor, and on that customer service call.

King Saul agreed to David's plea. It was either out of panic or stupidity, but who sends a boy to fight a giant? Maybe Saul had already resigned to the fact that they were going to have to surrender, so let us send the boy to get it over with quickly. Saul then gives David his armor. This is where David teaches us the sling mentality. David put the armor on but quickly took it off. It didn't feel right, it didn't fit, it wasn't the right clothing to wear. So David took off the armor and approached the Giant without any armor, just a sling and five smooth stones.

The world's methods and ways are often tried and trusted. They are like Saul's armor; they are there to protect you, for we live in a dog-eat-dog world where competitors are out there waiting for blood. These competitors will cut you down and fight at all costs until they win. The world teaches us a way to protect ourselves, trust very few people, and always look out for number one, so we put on armor so we will not get hurt.

David teaches us a different way. David's thought pattern is the God way. Why would I need armor to protect me when God protects me? Why do I need the methods and ways of the world when I have God's methods and ways? Why do I need to think like a defeatist when I am already fighting from victory, not for victory, because the battle is the Lord's?

David teaches us that with God on our side, we don't need armor, a spear, or a sword. All you need is a sling, for God is looking for someone who will say, "I'll go," and He will do the rest!

You more than likely know the rest of the story. David didn't need the five stones; just one was enough to kill Goliath. Israel wins, the Philistines flee, and David goes on to become Israel's hero, eventually to the distaste of a jealous Saul.

Many years later, Saul is so jealous of David that he pursues David to kill him. David flees and finds himself hiding in the caves of the hills of Israel. One day, while Saul is in pursuit, Saul needs the bathroom, so he goes into one of the caves to relieve himself. It's the same cave David is hiding in. Now is David's opportunity to take out the competition while Saul is vulnerable. The world would say to take him out to save yourself, but David refused, instead honoring the position of the King and just cutting a piece of the King's robe to show Saul that he is not going to act as anyone else would act and there is a different way, a way that does not listen to the world's methods, but instead seeks to honor God.

Again, at a later time, Saul is pursuing to kill David again. While Saul and his army slept at night in their camp, David and two of his best warriors crept into the king's camp and had the opportunity to take him out, but instead, he refused to kill the king and just took his spear as a warning to Saul, but even taking the spear left David feeling that he had done wrong. David did not listen to what others were telling him to do; he listened to his heart, and as he was a man after God's own heart, the feelings of his heart and the voice of his inner man were in sync with God.

The world would say destroy the competition if you want to make it to the top, but those like David, who understand that the battle is the Lord's, tell the story, "Allow the Lord take out the competition if He needs to." The way to the top is not to cut down others; it is to honor God.

David defeated a giant because he honored God. He honored God in the face of adversity. He took the high road when he had the opportunity to take the legs of those who wanted him dead. David had an anointing from God to be King, yet I'm sure hiding in the caves of the hills of Israel, he must have thought if it was ever going to happen. He may have wondered if choosing to honor Saul as the King was really the smartest action to take. However, when you see David's life as a whole, he made the right decision. David eventually became King because he honored God. David's family sat on the throne of Judah for generations after his death because he honored God.

The sling mentality thinks differently to this world. While the world tries to find new ways to win, those with the sling mentality turn and face God as they walk with the belief that the battle is the Lord's. He is the one who determines my steps. They believe that it doesn't matter if I have a spear, a sword, or a sling in my hand; with God on my side, this giant will come down! They face the difficulties of the marketplace, not trying to figure out the latest greatest new strategy and technique to win. Instead, they look at what God has put in their hand, and they move forward with what they have because the sling mentality reminds us daily that with God on our side, the end result is always victory, for the battle is the Lord's.

That day I sat in Chris's office, I didn't have the answers for him, for the methods of the world were sucking him dry. The energy and motivation he had shown in the previous months were gone. It was almost a Saul-like resignation that nothing was going to work. Chris was not a follower of Jesus; he wasn't open to hearing about how Jesus could lift the heavy burden, and Chris continued to struggle. I came out of that office feeling sorry for Chris but so thankful for the blessings God had poured on me. I was grateful that God had transformed my mind not to be so conditioned to kill the giants in my sales career with the armor the world had provided, but instead to first seek to honor Him and let Jesus take the burden. I look back at the many successes and deals won when I had a sling and a few stones. When you defeat a giant with God's help, you never want to go back to fighting giants with the world's help!

PRAYER FOR THE SLING

Father, in a world that will try to influence my decisions and direction, please help me keep an eye on the one who is my eternal help. When the world's methods and techniques seem attractive to me, keep my eyes fixed on you and the power you have in your hand. Help me to seek to follow you with a sling and a stone and not follow the world chasing after a sword and shield. I know with you, I can do all things because you are my strength; the battle belongs to you. Let us proceed into the battles I face, knowing I am not going forward in my own strength but that you are with me, my protection and defense. Giving me the mindset that I am fighting from victory, not for victory.

CHAPTER 4:
The Abundance Mentality

GROWING UP IN THE UNITED KINGDOM, WATER WAS ALWAYS IN ABUNdance. When you live in a climate where rain is in plenty, you rarely have to think of water conservation. A shortage of water for us was when it did not rain for two weeks, and the grass started to turn brown. We would hear stories of people without water in other parts of the world, but we could never truly understand their plight.

Last year, I traveled to Utah for the first time. I was blown away by the beauty, the cleanliness, and the majestic mountains everywhere you set your gaze. While Utah is a place of beauty, it is also one of the driest states in America. The people who live in this state are no strangers to water shortages and drought. I have had the privilege of developing friendships with many people who now live in South West Utah, and they will tell you, despite the beautiful surroundings, they are either living in drought or preparing for the next drought. They require significant snowfall in the winter in order to have enough water for the summer.

The people of Utah have to live constantly with a drought mentality, conserving as much water as possible, for the scarcity of water is real. It reminded me of the shortage of the sun in the United Kingdom. On a sunny day in Florida, you will see people inside with their air conditioning blowing, but across the pond, everyone clammers to go outside on a hot sunny day. Why? Because in Florida, there is an abundance of sunshine, but in England, there are only a limited number of sunny days, so enjoy it while it lasts. There is a phrase that I always think about when I see people outside on a blazing hot summer's day, "only mad dogs and Englishmen go out in the midday sun!"

When you live in a place of abundance, you do not have to worry about tomorrow, but when you live in a place of scarcity, tomorrow is a worry. When it comes to business, people often work in two different mindsets: the abundance mindset and the scarcity or drought mindset. Let me explain a little further.

Growing up, my father was a pastor in England. We did not have much money, and we lived on a very tight budget. I did not know how little my father was paid by our church until I went to college and found out I was able to get financial assistance due to being a low-income family. My parents hid our low income pretty well; even I was shocked that we were a low-income family. In reality, there was not an abundance of money, and we lived in our household with a scarcity mentality. We conserved everything because we did not have enough.

I remember reading the modern classic *Rich Dad Poor Dad* by Robert Kiyosaki and Sharon Lechter and thinking to myself, *My dad is indeed a poor dad!* We did not talk about money much because it brought so much stress. Over eighteen years ago, I married my beautiful bride, Raquel. It has been an incredible marriage filled with the usual highs and lows, seasons of pain, and seasons of joy. I have had to learn, and I am still developing, not to bring this scarcity mindset into our family that was so ingrained in me since I was a young child. Not that my parents were bad; they were wonderful parents and gave me the best upbringing. It is just when you live in scarcity, you believe the world is also scarce, and that becomes your worldview. I have learned that yes, we can talk about money at the dinner table, that money is a tool and not an evil we are a slave to, and that my words about money are shaping my son's worldview and also determining how money is viewed in our family.

When I landed my first sales job, I was two years out of college. I realized that my first job, which was in banking, was not going to pay enough; I needed to earn more. I left the bank and worked for a medical recruitment company. I soon discovered that I had some control over my income by how much I could sell. Every day, driving to the office, I would pray for sales. This was not just some ten-second prayer; this was hard intercession each day. My parents may not have talked about money at the dinner table, but we talked about prayer, and early in my childhood, I learned the power and effectiveness of prayer. The prayers worked. Sales would come in, and suddenly, I found myself earning more and more each month. However, I still lived with the scarcity mentality, and I did not realize that it had infiltrated my entire life.

I believed there were only a certain amount of opportunities available, and unless I could take them, someone else would. When I would see others be successful, while I was happy for them, deep down, I would believe their success would mean there would be less for me, so other people became my competition. I am a sports lover, and yes, I am competitive. I do not like losing, even a friendly round of golf with those I would consider good friends. I have come to understand that being competitive is not bad, but seeing others as your competitors can be crippling.

This mentality even surfaced when I planted our church. I wanted to be that pastor who constantly celebrated other churches and their pastors when they grew and were successful. Still, often, I would find myself trying to think of reasons why they were succeeding when there were seasons when we felt we were in a spiritual drought. God has had to deal with me, and it was not until I really started to let Romans 12 germinate within my soul that the healing took place. Feeling like there is always a chance that tomorrow the tide is going to turn and you are not going to have enough is no way to live, and it is not God's way to live!

Heather Monahan, the keynote speaker, podcaster, and author of *Overcome Your Villians*, regularly talks about how we need to stop viewing other people as our competitors. She says that there is no one like you, and what you bring into the world is like no other. Other people are not your competitors because they are not on the same level as you; they cannot bring to the world what you can bring. I like that! This is such a biblical principle. God has uniquely created each of us for his purpose. Others have a purpose, just as you have a purpose. You don't have the same purpose as the company down the street or that corporation that just took your biggest client. If you believe your purpose is the same as others, let us be honest! That is probably your own purpose for your life and not God's purpose for your life!

This brings us to the abundance mentality. Scarcity believes there is not enough; abundance believes there is more than enough. Did you catch that? Abundance is not just enough; making ends meet, we'll get by, no; abundance believes in *more* than enough.

The apostle Paul wrote about this to the Corinth church when he said in 2 Corinthians 9:8 (NLT), "And God will generously provide all you need. Then you will always have everything you need and plenty left over to share with others."

I wonder what my childhood would have been like if I had lived in this abundance Paul speaks about; if we would have had everything we needed with plenty left over. I wonder if that scarcity mentality that caused me to see others as my competitors or that stopped me from celebrating other people's success would not have even taken root in my mind. I wonder if I would have been a less threatened friend or pastor. I wonder if I missed out on more that God had for me because my scarcity mentality led to a close fist. An abundance mentality allows you to open your hands, and when you open your hands, it enables you to receive.

It is scriptures like these that have transformed my mind, and I pray they will transform your mind. You see, the abundance mentality believes that there is more than enough for everyone. This world is big enough for both of us, and God wants us both to prosper. Your success is not detrimental to my success. My purpose in this world is different from your purpose, and we are both needed to fulfill God's purpose.

The next time you lose a deal or a client to that firm down across town, instead of cussing them out and thinking of ways to bring them down, rejoice for them. There are plenty of other clients out there who want to do business with you. There are more sales to be made, more products to produce, more clients to take care of, and more people to help, for we live in a world of more than enough! Next time you are in a meeting, and someone brings up your competitors, try to introduce the Abundance principle. I guarantee many in that room will look at you like you have two heads because this type of thinking is so counter-cultural that those so aligned with the methods of the world's system just will not be able to understand it.

In 2021, when I decided to leave the insurance firm I had been a part of for so many years, it was hard. One of the reasons was because I do not like to be disliked. I'm a people pleaser, and one thing was for sure: I would become public enemy number one! In the weeks after resigning, I received letters from my previous employer's lawyers reminding me I had a non-solicitation agreement and any violation would result in them bringing suit against me.

Over the course of the next year, it seemed every time they lost a client, my new firm would get an email threatening to take me to court. That was probably not the case, but it seemed like that at the time. One fall morning, I was due to play in a charity golf tournament when I discovered my old firm was one of the mainline sponsors. I knew the owners would be there, and I didn't feel good about it. That morning, I sat down to pray, and this intense sense to pray for them and their firm came over me. I heard the words coming out of my mouth, "God bless them, increase their book of business, let them go from strength to strength." I couldn't believe what I was saying, but I knew it was the Holy Spirit teaching me a valuable lesson. Pray for those who persecute you and say all terrible things about you. Pray for your enemies. Trust me, praying for those who you know have issues with you and are trying to hurt you is not easy. You need all the grace and leading of the Holy Spirit to do it. Your nature wants them to suffer.

I went and played in the tournament. Unfortunately, I did not win, but it was a good time nonetheless. Later that evening, at the charity dinner, I saw one of my old employers going through the food line. I tried to say hello, but he basically turned away. Some of my old colleagues who I was close to were there also, and they didn't even dare look at me. It didn't feel great. Then, in the middle of dinner, an email came from one of the owners; they had decided to pursue legal action against us for violation of our agreement. I was stunned, shocked, and incredibly upset. Firstly, I knew I hadn't violated the agreement, but secondly, I had just prayed for them that morning!

I went home upset and prayed! I blamed the devil because he knew I had prayed for them to be blessed that morning. If there was ever a time I had wanted a prayer to be retracted, it was then. The long and short of it is that we never got a court summons, there were no legal proceedings, and now I'm not giving the devil that much credit. In fact, I wonder if it was God who orchestrated that whole day. I learned an incredible lesson: bless people even when they want to hurt you. They are not your competition; there is more than enough for all. The more you can cheer others on often has a direct effect on how much it seems God is cheering you on.

Before we close this chapter, you may have a question; I know I did! *Yes, Alex, I may not see others as my competitors, but others certainly see me as their competitor; there is a target on my back, and they are coming after me. How do I deal with those people?* Yes, that is true; just because you may have an abundance mentality does not mean others see the world this way. That is when I would encourage you to remember the sling mentality. The battle is the Lord's! When you honor Him, He will fight your battles! When you live to please Him, God will protect you. The abundance mentality is a mindset and a belief that pleases God. It pleases Him because you are now not living to just survive, but you are living to fulfill the purposes God had set for your life. When you celebrate others, you are allowing God to transform your mind by changing the way that you think, and this pleases God.

It is time to stop thinking about what others are doing. Stop worrying about your competitors. Do you think that God is worried? Of course not! He is the one who created the heavens and the earth with His voice. He made the stars and the moon with a word. He painted the colors of the rainbow and formed the landscapes of the earth. Your God took some dust and created a perfect human body; He breathed life into that body, and it came to life. He is the one who put the fish in the sea and caused the flowers to grow. As God told Job in Job 38:4 (NIV), "Where were you when I laid the foundations of the earth?" Do you think that your God is not big enough and mighty enough to fight your battles? If He can bring the rain to water the earth, then don't you think He is able to provide all your needs and more? Allow your mind to be transformed from scarcity to abundance, and watch as you will discover the God of *more than enough*.

PRAYER FOR ABUNDANCE

Father, help me to see the world through your eyes—a world of plenty where a scarcity mindset does not limit my thinking. Help me to look to you when I feel like I will not have enough and to celebrate with others when they receive what I want. Make yourself known to me, the great El Shaddai, the one who is sufficient and more than enough. Meet my needs, let my storehouses be full, and the vats of my life overflow.

CHAPTER 5:

The Ambassador Mentality

ENGLAND IN THE 1990S SAW A SHARP DECLINE IN CHURCH ATTENdance. Churches saw their membership decrease as a post-modern secular culture infiltrated the nation. This wave of change in values resulted in a great divide between church and regular life. When I graduated High School in the mid-nineties, I was one of only four people in our school of over 1,600 students who would identify themselves as bornagain Christians.

Living in what would now be called in many circles a post-Christian culture meant that I started to stand out from the rest. Throughout my university years and at the start of my career, there were many times when the values of my faith clashed with the values of the culture we lived in. It was early in my career that I discovered the ambassador mindset, and it has been something that is always at the forefront of my mind whenever I walk into an office, boardroom, event, or lunch appointment.

Before I talk about what this ambassador mentality is, allow me to give a little more clarity as to why this is such a critical mindset, yet so many Christ followers miss it. At the age of twenty-six, I moved to Springfield, Missouri. It was a culture shock. Coming from my hometown of Wolverhampton, England, which was as diverse a city as it comes. Different races, different nationalities, different beliefs, different levels of income, and even different football (soccer for my American readers) teams. Being different was the norm! Springfield was the complete opposite. There were very few people who were not American. I had read a report while I lived there which, to be honest, I do not know how true it was, but it seemed accurate, in which it said that Springfield was in the top ten of the "whitest" cities in America. My wife is Hispanic. We always joke that when we moved away from Springfield, a quarter of its diversity moved as well. What's more, almost everyone was a Christian, and if they didn't identify as Christian, they grew up in church and had more knowledge of church than most non-believers I had ever met. There was an incredible cultural difference between post-Christian Wolverhampton and Bible-belt Springfield. However, I did notice one similarity, and this was amongst the church-going Christians; it appeared that the most spiritual people became pastors and leaders in the churches while everyone else did what would be called "regular jobs."

There was almost an underlying belief that the pastor did the ministry, and everyone else paid their tithes, gave their offerings, and volunteered in roles that were a little lower than the real ministry work the pastors did. There was a divide between the vocational ministers (the paid staff and pastors) and lay people (everyone else). Once in a while, one of the lay people would show themselves to be very faithful and spiritual and receive the opportunity to fill in for the vocational pastors, but if you were really spiritual, then God had a call on your life to work for a church.

This just seemed off to me. When I became a bi-vocational church planter, this belief was blown to pieces. In the ten years of being both in the marketplace and in the church as a Senior Pastor, the marketplace gave me some of the most significant opportunities to tell people about Jesus. When you look at the life of Jesus, it was not in the synagogue or the temple where He did His most remarkable ministry; it was in the streets, in the farmer's fields, on the fishermen's boats, and in the marketplace that He spent most of His time and showed His power. The western church has a bad habit of taking the most spiritual and the best leaders and bringing them inside of the four walls of the church to help create better church services. Instead, I am a believer that it would be more beneficial to help resource these people and send them back out into the marketplace where they can make an even greater difference for the kingdom of heaven.

My friend Harry Plack is a man you want to listen to when he talks. He is a man of wisdom. Harry owns a successful local CPA firm and is the author of the book *Get Your Life Back*. It doesn't take long after meeting Harry before you know that Harry loves Jesus! It also will not be long before you hear Harry say, "We are all ministers and pastors whether a church pays us or not. The church I pastor also happens to be a CPA firm; this is what God has given me, and I must steward it well and use it for God's kingdom." Wow! Talk about a man who gets it. A church doesn't pay him, nor did he go to a Theological Seminary, but I can guarantee you this: Harry is living his purpose, and he is not any less spiritual or have any less a call of God on his life than your local pastor. Harry was called to be a minister, and it's just through the instrument of being an incredible CPA instead of a seasoned preacher.

The ambassador mentality is simply this: you are the representative of Jesus wherever you may go. Just like an ambassador is their country's representative to the country they are commissioned to, you are God's ambassador in the business, workplace, school, or non-profit you find yourself in.

The apostle Paul wrote about this principle in his second book to the Corinthians:

> *And God has given us the task of reconciling the world to Him. For God was in Christ, reconciling the world to himself, no longer counting people's sins against them. And He gave us this wonderful message of reconciliation. So we are Christ's ambassadors; God is making His appeal through us.*
>
> — 2 Corinthians 5:19–20 (NLT, paraphrased)

Paul gives us a task, which is to reconcile the world to God. To reconcile means to restore a relationship. When you thought your job was to build that business, hit those goals, implement that project, or manage that team, it wasn't. Your real task was to reconcile people to God. It was just through the instrument of managing people, building a business, or providing exceptional work to your employers that God wanted you to do it.

Paul tells us that we are Christ's ambassadors. Just like the ambassador of a country speaks and represents their country to foreign officials, so too, we are Christ's ambassadors to a broken and lost world that is foreign to the grace and love of Christ. We are the connection between them and Christ.

The Gospels show us a beautiful example of this task Paul gives to us. In Matthew 10 and Luke 9, Jesus gathers together His disciples. The Bible tells us that Jesus gave them the power to cast out demons and heal diseases, then He sent them out. This is a picture of who we are as Christ's ambassadors. He has given us His power and has sent us out into the marketplace. In Luke 10:2 (NLT), Jesus tells a greater number of His followers, "The harvest is great, but the workers are few." Notice that Jesus did not send out His disciples for them to bring all the people back to church. No, Jesus sent them out as if He was also going out with them.

Not too long ago, I spoke to a young professional who wanted advice on being more confident throughout some of the business meetings he was involved in. He told of how he felt inadequate as the people in these meetings were more experienced, more intelligent, and better equipped than he was. He felt he needed something of value to bring. Knowing this young professional was a Christ follower, I could present the ambassador mentality, and he would receive it well. I told him that when he walked into the room, he could bring what no one else in that room could bring. While the others brought the experience, the intelligence, the know-how, the statistics, and the creativity, he was able to bring something so much more significant. When he walked into the room, he was bringing Jesus into that room, and when Jesus is in the room, it makes all the difference.

This young man had never considered himself an ambassador for Christ before, and this new empowered mindset made all the difference for him. He felt more confident and knew he had more significant value to bring than he ever imagined he could bring. This was not just a moral boost for this young man but a life-changing moment. For the first time in his life, he felt the purpose and calling of God upon him; there was a higher reason to work than to make money and build a career. Now, he was on a mission to reconcile the world to Christ.

This can be your story as well. It is not just paid staff at a church or para-church ministry that God has called. God has a purpose for you, even in the marketplace. That purpose is to be the one to bring Jesus into the room! You are an ambassador for Christ, and He has empowered you to do His work, just as Jesus gave power to His disciples before He sent them out. Jesus desires to empower you, so when you walk into that boardroom, you attend that networking event, you step onto the shop floor, you log into that video conference call, you walk out onto that stage, you step into your office building, or you enter your client's place of business, you, yes you are the one bringing Jesus into the mix, and when Jesus shows up people are changed, and reconciliation to God begins to occur. You will walk into many rooms that have never allowed Jesus to come in, but when you come in, you are bringing Jesus with you. Every room that you walk into should be different because you are there! You have value because you are bringing Jesus with you.

God has placed you in the environments you live and work in for a reason. Allow him to work in and through you, and your life will take on a whole new meaning. Many people talk about being the hands and feet of Jesus when there is a missions outreach at church. However, you are more than just hands and feet every day. To the people you are meeting and interacting with, you are the very embodiment of Christ to them. The Holy Spirit resides within you, so when you step over the threshold, not only did you step into the room, but the very life, power, and reconciling love of Christ stepped into the room. Do not underestimate what you bring!

This should also be a good reminder that people are also watching us. When we step into the room self-focused, stressed out, and unaware of our actions, we show a lousy representation of Christ. Sometimes, especially when our daily lives are spent in the marketplace, we must self-check ourselves regularly. Am I portraying the fruits of the spirit? Am I loving? Showing joy? Walking in peace? Patient? Kind? Longsuffering? Gentle? Controlling my mouth, body, email, and actions? Remember, we are ambassadors of Christ. When we walk into the room, what impression of Jesus will they receive?

The next meeting or event you attend. Before you walk through those doors, take a moment to think about who will be in that room. Who needs the reconciling love of Jesus? Who needs peace in their lives? Whose life is falling apart? Who is looking for something greater? I promise that this mindset change turns boring, mundane meetings into ones of purpose and significance. You are not just there to discuss the latest IT install or the quarterly budget. You are there to minister and to live out your calling. For Jesus is with you, and where He is, there is a desire to reconcile people to Himself.

PRAYER TO BE AN AMBASSADOR

Father, help me to represent you well wherever I go. Help me to understand that when I walk into a room, you are also with me. May I steward well your presence that goes before me, beside me, and behind me. Help me to keep a godly countenance about me where people see the presence of Jesus in me. Guide me to make decisions that will honor you, not decisions that will just benefit me. As I walk in the authority you have given me, let my life be pleasing in your sight.

CHAPTER 6:

The Favored Mentality

HAVE YOU EVER FOUND YOURSELF IN A PLACE WHERE YOU WONDERED how you even got there? You won that account that you had no right winning. You got that meeting that you were told was impossible to get. You got endorsed by your industry's experts when you knew there were better products they could have supported. Let's scale back a little; you were shown unbelievable kindness by your employer, and you were taken under the wing of that business superstar who said they would help mentor you. You got into that college you did not think you would ever get into. I could go on and on. There are times in life when we just have to acknowledge that it wasn't me who got me there; it had to be God! While I am not going to try to teach a gospel that tells you that the more you give, then in return, God will give back to you. This type of gospel and teaching is just inaccurate.

The truth is that as sinners who have fallen short of God's glorious standard, we do not deserve anything. However, those who have surrendered their life and will to Jesus Christ have discovered the abundant grace that follows those who believe in the life, death, resurrection, and second coming of Jesus. We talked at length about this in Chapter 2 when I introduced the grace mentality. However, if you can recall back to that chapter, grace is underserved kindness. God pours out His kindness, not because of what you have done; it is all because of who He is and what He has done. Did you know that God delights in you, faults and failures and all, and because He delights in you, He desires to pour His kindness out on you? Another way of explaining this kindness is the word favor! Grace is the unmerited favor upon your life.

This favor is not just to save you from your sins, but this favor can and will if you surrender to God's ways, flow through every fiber of your life. From your family to your health. From your finances or your career. Now, along the way, we will suffer at times. There will be moments when you will question God and seasons of pain. That is life. We live in a fallen, broken world that needs reconciling to God. One of the consequences of this sin is that life at times will be hard; there is no question about that. However, when you capture a taste of the favor of God, your eyes are opened to the unrelenting kindness God pours out on your life each and every day.

A few months back, I was riding through central Florida with my brother-in-law, Obed. He was a pastor in Lakeland, Florida, for almost twenty years. Just over a year ago, he felt led by the Holy Spirit to pass on his church's leadership baton. This is never an easy decision for a pastor, and often, it takes a lot of bravery and wisdom to admit that God is asking you to stand down. Obed knew he was heading into a season in which his family needed him, so he informed his board and then, some months later, the rest of the church's congregation. The question most people asked Obed was a question I was very familiar with as I had, and I still get asked regularly, "What are you doing next? Are you going to pastor another church?" For Obed, he didn't know what was next. All he knew was that God had given him new orders: take a break! In a perfect world, it would be nice to take a long extended vacation, but like most of us, Obed had bills he had to pay.

Obed found employment pretty quickly and joined a landscaping team as part of his county's school system. I have so much respect for Obed's humility. Many leaders would see a job on a landscaping crew in hot central Florida as below them, but not Obed. He went from leading hundreds to being told to pick weeds. I can not help but feel that God loves this attitude and humility. It wasn't even two weeks into his job that Obed got promoted. He was transferred to the best team and found the kindness of his foreman. Within nine months of faithfully doing his job, he was recommended to apply for a senior foreman position and got the job. There have been many who have worked on those teams for years but have never had the opportunity to put their name forward for the foreman position.

Talking in the car that day, Obed was telling me all about this new promotion, and I just could not help but smile. I told Obed, "Listen, just because you are not pastoring at the moment does not mean the blessings and favor of God on your life have gone. No, wherever you go, whatever you do, when you are faithful to the Lord, He goes with you. Of course, you got that job so quickly; of course, you got that promotion while others have been waiting for years because the hand of God is in your life, and you have the favor of God. You will be blessed more than others because the favor does not leave you."

I am confident that Obed will soon be back in some vocational ministry role; that is his calling, and he is so gifted in what he does. I am also sure the favor of God will be with him, just like it was in his last church and just like it is now while he is working in the school system. When you lean into God's grace, favor always follows. God's favor isn't limited to when you finally make it, living out the purpose of your life. God's favor also is not limited to maybe a season that has already come and gone. God's favor is for now and follows you wherever you go.

There was a man in the Bible who had his life chronicled. His life gives evidence that no matter what season of life you are in, when you stay close to God, favor follows. This man is Joseph, the kid who had ten older brothers. From a young age, he found favor from his father. Genesis 37:3 (NIV) tells us, "Now Israel (Jacob his father) loved Joseph more than any of his other sons because he had been born to him in his old age; and he made an ornate robe from him."[1] There are three principles to note about the favor that was on Joseph.

The first is that he was loved or favored more than his other brothers. This can, at times, be hard to understand. Why are some people favored more than others? What if someone is favored more than me? Does it mean they are more spiritual than me? Does God love them more? The answer to that is no! God's grace abounds, but His favor is not just because He

---

1 Text within parentheses added by the author.

wants to bless you. I do believe that God wants to bless you because He loves you, but often, the favor of God is evident upon someone's life because God is using that favor to fulfill a purpose in or through that person. I have seen seasons of incredible favor but also seasons that felt like Murphy and his brothers moved into my home; what could go wrong went wrong. What we need to understand is that God is working, and at times, it is through blessing, and at other times it is through hardship. God was going to use the favor upon Joseph to save a nation.

The second principle is that Joseph was not the reason He had found favor. This is an important one and takes us back to the grace mentality. It is not because of you; it is all because of Christ. Joseph found favor with Jacob because he was his child in old age. This is important. Joseph's mother was Rachel. She was the girl who had stolen Jacob's heart. Jacob loved Rachel dearly, but she was not able to have children. Jacob had another wife, Rachel's sister Leah, and a few lady friends; in biblical language, they are called concubines. He was able to have children with all these other ladies, but the one he really wanted a child with, Rachel, was unable to. One day, God remembered Rachel's plight and allowed her womb to live. Joseph was the gift of this miracle. You see, it was not because Joseph was this amazing young man that he found favor; it was because of who his mother was. The quickest way to walk out of the favor of God is for you to take the credit for why you are receiving the kindness of God. It is not because of what you have done. I'll say it again: it is all because of what Christ has already done!

The third principle to note is that Joseph received a gift. It was a coat of many colors that made his brothers angry with jealousy. There is an enormous blessing to God's favor, and that is that you will receive what you did not work for. I have had to learn many times over that when God gives, you receive, you accept, you say thank you, and then you give thanksgiving to God. Too often, people stub the favor of God because they feel they do not deserve what they are being offered.

The story of Joseph evolves into being thrown into a pit with the idea of being left to die by his jealous brothers. In that pit, he received the favor of God when Ishmaelite traders agreed to purchase him as a slave. These Ishmaelite traders journeyed to Eygpt, where he was purchased by the captain of the Kings' guard, Potiphar. Genesis tells us that Joseph succeeded in everything he did, and Potiphar noticed him, so Joseph got promoted. It does not matter what environment you find yourself in; God's favor will always allow you to rise to the top when you honor Him. The problem with favor, though, is that others become attracted by it. The more people who are attracted to you, the greater the temptation to walk away from the one who is blessing you.

This temptation came to Joseph. Potiphar's wife took a liking to this young, handsome boy. Remember, his mother was the beautiful Rachel; he probably had his mother's genes, and the Bible basically tells us that he was eye candy to the Egyptian ladies. When Joseph refused the advances of Potiphar's wife, it felt like God had deserted him. Joseph was thrown into prison for accused rape. However, this again shows the favor of God. Remember, the favor of God is not just so we can be blessed. It is to fulfill the purposes of God. Joseph was not thrown into any prison; he was thrown into the King's prison. Just because it was the King's prison does not mean the environment was any more pleasant, but what it did mean was that there were people in that prison with influence. They had close proximity to the King, and that is where God was taking Joseph to an audience with the King.

You may find yourself in a work environment that feels anything like the favor of God is in your life, but I do not believe you are there by chance. It is often in the most distasteful environments that God's favor shines on us, which connects us with the purposes and the palaces that God has planned for our lives. This was Joseph's story. In that dark, dirty prison, he interpreted two dreams that were fulfilled. Years later, one of those prisoners who was employed as the King's cupbearer had been pardoned and restored to his position. As he worked in close proximity next to the King, the cupbearer heard of a disturbing dream the King had dreamt. No one in the palace could tell the King the meaning of the dream. Then the cupbearer remembered Joseph, and before you knew it, Joseph was standing in front of the King, interpreting his dream. The result is that a famine was predicted, and Joseph was put in charge of the entire land of Eygpt. Talk about favor! Who goes from a nasty prison cell to the governor in one day?

There are so many lessons we could learn from the story of Joseph, but one we have to know if we are going to be a Christ follower in a corporate jungle is the favor that was on Joseph while he stood before the King of Egypt was the same favor that was on him as he found favor while in the prison cells of the king's palace. And the favor in the prison cell was the same favor he found in Potiphar's house. The favor he found in

Potiphar's house was the same favor he found in the pit where he was supposed to die. The same favor he found in the pit was the same one he found in his father's gift of a coat. The favor looked different; for Joseph, it certainly felt different, but it was the same favor because it came from the same source, that was his God in heaven!

When you live your life according to the Word of God and dedicate your life to His purposes, do not be surprised if you find yourself standing before Kings. Do not be surprised if you receive gifts you did not earn; do not be surprised when a promotion comes your way. However, do not blame yourself when you find yourself at the bottom of a pit, or you receive false accusations, or you get given what may seem like a demotion. When the favor of God is on you, it always results in God's purposes being fulfilled, and as Jeremiah 29:11 (NIV) comforts us, God tells us, "For I know the plans I have for you, declares the Lord, plans to prosper you and not to harm you, plans to give you hope and a future."

When you walk in grace, stay close to the Father, and trust in God with your sling instead of the armor the world depends on. When you have an abundance mindset and understand your role as an ambassador, there is a favor that follows you. I have heard on many occasions people say, "If you follow the world's methods, you will reap the world's rewards, but if you follow God's ways, you will reap His kingdom's rewards!" What a powerful yet truthful statement. We are not to walk into our businesses or workplaces with arrogance; we are to keep ourselves humble, but we should walk and work with the belief that I am not doing this in my own strength. I am walking in the grace and power of Jesus, and the result is that favor will surround me wherever I go.

Think about the places, opportunities, and people that have come and gone in your life. Do you see how God opened those doors and allowed you to walk down that road? Look long enough, and you will see God's hand upon your life, giving you favor to walk through doors you had no right walking through. You will see how God supplied the resources to be able to expand or make a difference. You will see a pattern in your life emerge, which will show that God is using you for His purposes and that when God has placed favor on your life, He uses it to fulfill His purpose. What an incredible thought this is. God is using me for His purposes! When God could have used anyone and anything to fulfill His purpose, He chooses to partner with you. How does that make you feel? I hope it fills your life with joy and expectation for the favor God is currently pouring out on you.

PRAYER FOR FAVOR

Father, I thank you for the favor you have poured out into my life. I am in awe of the doors you have opened for me and the people I have been able to have an audience with. Without your favor, I would have been struggling to find opportunities to walk into, but with your favor poured out on me, I have received what I did not deserve. I have walked through doors I did not open, been on appointments I did not set, and received kindness from others that I did not deserve. I recognize that your favor is great, and I do not take it for granted or believe I am entitled to it. I am thankful that you have blessed me.

Continue to shower me with blessings, and as I have received the favor of God, also grant me the favor of men.

CHAPTER 7:

The Right Order Mentality

MY SON EVAN IS A CHILD OF ROUTINE. HE LIKES TO KNOW THE EXACT plan for the day, and when something is out of order, he gets frustrated and is not shy about telling his parents this is not the right way. Routine, habits, and order help us to stay in sync with the world. While I think my son has a slight case of OCD, when I think about some of the routines in my life, when I do them out of order, something does not seem right.

    I enjoy not just playing golf but also practicing and studying golf. I am that eternal optimist who one day still believes he will shoot under par for eighteen holes even though time and age are not on my side. One golf tip I learned early through this golf journey was to adopt a pre-shot routine. What that means is that before I hit the ball, I have a few checks I do before I make the golf swing. For me, it basically is the same every time. I stand about 6 feet behind the ball, take a practice swing, then draw an imaginary line between where I want the ball to land and the ball in front of me. Then I find a spot on the ground about a yard in front of the ball that is on that imaginary line; I keep my eyes fixed on that spot, then I address the ball and aim my club at the spot. Then, I transfer my weight a few times between my left and right foot until I feel perfect balance. I pause, and then I swing. It's not a perfect golf shot every time, but let me tell you, the percentages are tremendously higher when I go through my pre-shot than when I get lazy and do not go through the process of hitting a good golf shot.

There is something about doing it right that allows the rest to fall into line. There has been much study on how powerful habit-making is to human success. *The Power of Habit* by Charles Duhigg and *Atomic Habits* by James Clear are two of the most outstanding books I have read on the formation and results of habit forming. Both these books will change your daily routine after you read them. While they both speak at length about the importance of creating good habits, these books speak to more of a focused approach to specific tasks and daily routines. I want to touch on a wider approach to these routines briefly; I call it "the right order mentality." This is more of a 10,000-foot view of your life than lasering in on certain aspects of your life.

I have heard Dave Ramsey, the founder of Ramsey Solutions and radio star of the Dave Ramsey Show, say on many occasions, "Show me your bank statement, and I will tell you what you value most." What Dave is saying is that where you spend your money shows those portions of your life that are most important to you. If that is true for money, then if we were to take a 10,000-foot-high view of your life and look down on your time, money, values, decisions, and behaviors, what would it show us?

I thoroughly enjoy it, and I am thankful to live in the United States of America. There are opportunities I have found in the USA that I could never have imagined finding elsewhere. However, there is no feeling like flying home to the United

Kingdom. When it is not raining, Britain is one of the most beautiful places you will find on planet Earth, well I think so anyway. When you come into British airspace and look out of the airplane window, you start to see the beauty of the British countryside. As you look down, it almost looks like a patchwork blanket, for the fields are all separated by hedge-lined fences, and many fields are different colors. If you drive on the roads of Britain, you get a feeling there is no rhyme or reason to the flow of roads. Unlike in most American cities, where roads are straight from North to South or East to West, British roads are curved and winding. However, when you look down out of the airplane window, you see that there is a pattern and an order to the roads. The roads follow the pattern of the fields. It is the shape of the property owned by the landowner that determines the direction of the road. From 10,000-plus feet, you see it; there is an order.

For the Christian business leader, what order and pattern would others see if they viewed your life from 10,000 feet? I want to present to you an order that not only do I believe is biblical but also an order to your life that allows God to work in and through you as you have never experienced before. It is an order that many talk about, but in truth, many do not have. An order and pattern to your life that when approached with the next decision, opportunity, or testing moment, you can stop like a golfer, checking their pre-shot routine and going through the pattern to ensure everything is in order before you proceed.

THE GOD-FIRST MENTALITY

If you indulge yourself in a Christian community for long enough, you will hear a few cliché statements over and over again. One of these statements is God first. What it means is that we are putting God first in our lives. The reason I say it is a cliché statement is because it is so easy to say, but very few actually live out this principle in their life. Many believe that putting God first is just living by Judeo-Christian values, belonging to a church community, and paying tithes to your local church. While I commend all the above, there is a difference between living a Christian lifestyle and putting God first.

Just think about that statement: God first! That is a powerful statement. When I read my Bible, I see story after story of people who failed to put God first. When the tough decisions came, there were countless accounts of how people put themselves first before they lived out the principle of God first. Adam, Abraham, Isaac, Jacob, Moses, Joshua, Samson, Saul, David, Solomon, Jonah, Peter, and so on. Person after person who had moments when they thought about how the decisions before them would affect their own lives before they thought about God first.

The truth of the matter is it is so much easier to say God first than it is to live out a God-first life. There will always be moments when you will put your own feelings and emotions ahead of what God desires; that is a result of sin in this world and living in sinful bodies. This is why grace is just so important, and we have to ensure we never lose the wonder of the incredible value of the grace that has been bestowed onto our lives. However, I do believe there are a few priorities we can put in place that will help us to live a God-first life. A

God-first life is not meant to deprive us of the good things in life; it is there to give us the best life. A God-first life will always be a more fulfilling and rewarding life than a me-first life. A God-first life is filled with more peace, more patience, more contentment, more joy, more lasting relationships, and more hope than any me-first life I have ever witnessed. Why? Because, as Jeremiah 29:11 tells us, God has plans for us, and they are the best plans.

Jesus understood that humanity has a scarcity mentality, not an abundance mentality. We have this habit of storing up what we have. Now, don't get me wrong, saving is good, putting aside for retirement is wise, and having a surplus is just prudent, but far too many people worry so much about tomorrow that their fear of tomorrow dictates their decisions. I had this same issue on that hot July afternoon when I was stressing about my employment at my insurance agency. Jesus, therefore, spoke to this. He said,

> *So don't worry about these things, saying, 'What will we eat? What will we drink? What will we wear?' These things dominate the thoughts of unbelievers, but your heavenly Father already knows all your needs. Seek the Kingdom of God above all else, and live righteously, and He will give you everything you need.'*
>
> — Matthew 6:31–33 (NLT)

Jesus gives us three commands: seek the kingdom, live righteously, and receive from Him. This is how you live a God-first life. Seek, live, and receive from Him. When you do this, your business, team, department, or organization will see a transformation like never before. The world's customs are to seek out the experts, live to be the best, and receive a paycheck. I do not know about you, but the world's customs do not seem as fail-proof as they market themselves to us. When you submit to the world's economy, you get rewarded by the world's economy, but when you submit to God's economy, you are rewarded by God's economy. The world's economy fails every seven or so years. God's economy has never failed!

When you have a God-first mentality, you put His Word first. That means you choose to study His Word, the Bible. This does not mean you need to go out and get a seminary degree. The Bible was written in stories, letters, and songs. It was not meant to be a mystery to be decoded; it was meant to be read, understood, and followed. Make it a daily habit to not just read your Bible but a daily habit to breathe in the words of the Bible, whether that is through a reading plan, a chapter-a-day routine, or just a few verses a day. "For the word of God is living and powerful, and sharper than any two-edged sword, piercing even to the division of soul and spirit, and of joints and marrow, and is a discerner of the thoughts and intents of the heart" (Hebrews 4:12, NKJV).

When you breathe in the words of the Bible, or as Ezekiel was told to do in Ezekiel 3:1, to eat the words, it is not just information that you receive. Hebrews tells us that it bridges the gap between the soul and spirit; it then divides what is earthly from what is heavenly. The word of God transforms our thinking; it gives wisdom, creates clarity, and changes our perspective. Make it a daily habit, before you have to make any decision of substance, that first you have "eaten" the Word of God.

When you have a God-first mentality, you put His worship first. Going back to the grace mentality, when you understand it is all because of Christ, not because of you, it then becomes very easy to worship your creator. It was not by accident that when the disciples asked Jesus how to pray when Jesus gave the prayer model known as the Lord's Prayer, it began with worship, "Our Father, who art in heaven, hallowed by your name."

Worship in modern Christian circles has so often been pigeonholed into music and songs. The reason for this is song is such a great way to express thankfulness and emotion, but there are so many more ways to worship. To worship basically means to bring your worth! I have a feeling that far too many Christians are bringing all their worth to their vocational job and leaving very little to bring to God. What do you have of worth to bring to God? Is your time worth anything to you? Are your resources and money worth much to you? What are your plans, dreams, and goals worth to you? What about your abilities and giftedness? How about the words that come out of your mouth?

I have changed my daily routine over the last few years, and the results have been incredible. I now start my work day later than most. I used to start my day at 8 a.m. most days. I jumped right in, knowing each day I had so much to get through. If I didn't start early, then the day would get away from me, and I would be more behind. However, I now start my day later than others when it comes to work. Before I answer an email, take a phone call, reply to a text, or walk into a meeting, there is now a pre-work routine I have adopted. I sit in my office, open my Bible, and spend the next 30 to 45 minutes breathing in the words of the Bible, bringing my worth to God and then asking God for wisdom and clarity. You see, time for me during working hours is most valuable to me, and I have decided that God gets my time before my clients. The results have astounded me. The stress of time management has gone. It feels like each day, I have more and more time available while becoming more productive and efficient. Let me tell you that when you seek the kingdom of God first, then Jesus takes care of the rest.

When you have a God-first mentality, you put His house first. I have always had a love for the church. One of my favorite verses in the whole Bible is found in Psalm 23:6 (NLT), when David wrote, "Surely your goodness and unfailing love will pursue me all the days of my life, and I will live in the house of the Lord forever." David's passion for God's house is evident throughout his life. From the religious reforms he made while ruling Israel to his dream of building a temple for the Lord. Whether you are a pastor, a small business owner, a W2 employee, an entrepreneur, or a CEO of a Fortune 500 company, if you are a follower of Jesus, then a passion for God's house is a must.

There are far too many people who do not believe that church is a requirement when it comes to putting God first. Yet, how can you put God first without enjoying His house and His people? It would be like saying your family is your priority, but you rarely step foot in the home of your spouse and children. Your actions would say that your family is not a priority, for when you are passionate about something, you give it your attention, time, and your worth!

Many pastors and church staff members find it hard to understand the weekly and monthly rhythms of the average business person. While churches desire full participation in all the weekly activities they provide, from Bible studies to prayer services to small groups and the monthly potluck, there is often a tension that exists for the marketplace leader. I get it! I am going to give you a gift, and that gift is this: you do not have to be at everything your church wants you to be! This is not a knock on your pastor or your ministry leader, but it is very hard to understand the rhythms of the business leader if you have never been a business leader. In the same way, as a business leader, you will never be able to understand the weight and stress of being a pastor unless you have been a pastor. Your calling as a business leader means you are an ambassador of Jesus to the marketplace. It is there in the marketplace that your presence is required. However, this does not mean that you can excuse non-commitment to your local church.

A God-first life always sees the importance and incredible value of the local church. It teaches us Godly submission, it teaches us humility, it teaches us to be a servant, it teaches us spiritual community. In my eyes, there are few things more powerful than a successful C-suite executive sitting down on a Sunday morning with a group of kids or students as their Sunday school or student leader. Do you know what that says to the next generation? God's house is a priority. I do not know what you may have to do to your schedule or what opportunities you have to say no to, but make Sunday a priority to be in church, serve in your church, and watch the blessings and favor of God overflow in your life.

My pastor and good friend, Wade, founder of Freedom Church, Bel Air, MD, needed to raise funds when he started Freedom Church. At the time, it was called Way of Life

Community. Not having a massive amount of resources, the church was unable to pay him a salary, so he started a construction company, helping construct steel-framed structures so he could pay his bills while he got the church off the ground. In those early years, as the majority of church planters will testify, the church grew at a very small rate. A few additions here and there, but the struggle was real. However, as the church was progressing much slower than he had anticipated, his construction company was growing like wildfire. Through the growth of the business, he was able to employ staff who could work on the business and also help with the church at the same time. The favor of God was on him. They were prospering in the marketplace while trying to build and grow a church. Wade is a savvy businessman whose heart is always for the church. He did not let the blessing of God in his company turn his attention from building the church of Jesus Christ. One day, Wade felt the overwhelming voice of God that soon it would be time to give up the business so that he could turn all his attention to the church. This voice grew louder and louder each day. One day, Wade found himself in a room that most business owners could only dream of being in. His company was involved in a large project that was being funded by the royal family of one of the Middle Eastern countries. This oil-rich family was ready to invest more money than you could count into the United States. The leading players in this project were invited into a meeting where a delegation from this royal family would join them to cast their vision. Wade said that the leader of this delegation was one of the strongest leaders he had ever met. The respect he commanded was undeniable. As everyone in the room was in awe of the opportunity to be so close to an influential person, Wade's mind was elsewhere. This was an opportunity of a lifetime for his company; it could open many doors, but all he could think about while he was in that room was the church. Everyone else in that room could not believe they were there. Wade couldn't wait to get out of that room. God had put a passion within him for Freedom Church that was greater than rubbing shoulders with the Crown Prince of an oil-rich nation. This is what it means to live in a God-first mentality.

Not long after this, Wade made moves to transition out of his company into his church role full-time; Freedom Church now boasts four campuses, three in Maryland and one in Kenya. It attracts over 3,000 worshippers each week and is growing like never before. Wade has attracted some of the most gifted leaders to join him in moving the mission of Freedom forward. He has no regrets and makes an incredible difference in the kingdom of God.

You don't have to give up your business to have a God-first mentality, but I challenge you to seek an audience with God before an audience with the world's influencers. Give what is of worth to you unto your savior before you use it to make your life easier, and consume His Word before you seek out the wisdom of the world's experts. When you do that, Jesus gives you a promise: He will take care of the rest.

THE FAMILY-SECOND MENTALITY

Once you fully commit to God genuinely being first, every other part of your life starts to fall into alignment. The first aspect is a change in your mentality when it comes to your family. The world will tell you to take care of yourself first; you are the most important, and no one else will take care of you. I can see the world's thinking; it makes sense, but it just is not biblical and not how the kingdom of God functions. A person who is in alignment with the purposes of God understands that their family is their second priority.

For the business leader: before you are anything in the marketplace, you are a leader in your home. Your first and most important priority is to lead your home. This is the most challenging and rewarding environment you will ever lead. At our church, we never baptized babies. We believe that baptism is a public declaration to the world of the transforming and saving grace of Jesus being done on the inside of you. We believe that baptism follows salvation. Therefore, baptism in water could only be practiced once a person is old enough to make a personal decision to follow Christ. What we do, though, is dedicate babies. We would dedicate them to God, pray over them, and pray for their parents. This is the act of asking God to watch over these babies as they grow and also for wisdom for their parents to parent them according to biblical principles. One of the statements I would make, especially to Fathers, but this also includes Mothers as well, is this: "You are the priest of your home; a priest cannot save or forgive the sins of your child, but a priest creates the environment where God can be accessed. In your home, create an environment where Jesus resides, where they experience Jesus, for it is Jesus who saves them. You are to lead them to Jesus."

Business leader, that is your most important job. Before you lead that organization, before you manage that team, before you make that sale, before you step into the boardroom, before you make that strategic decision, you are to lead your family.

The world will tell you that success is making money, having influence, and climbing the career ladder. In the kingdom of God, I believe success is a family that lives in an environment that regularly experiences Jesus. Your children have to make their own decision for Jesus; they may reject Him, but your job is not to save them. It is to lead them to Jesus, then Jesus does the rest.

Several years ago, I changed my schedule to adopt this family-second mentality. As I have mentioned previously, golf is a love of mine. It is my outlet. Soccer used to be my outlet, but old knees and ankles do not allow me the opportunity to play soccer and still walk. Saturday mornings were my time. I would leave the house early on Saturday for my tee time and be finished by 1 p.m. However, it was a bone of contention in our house. Sundays were dedicated to church, and Monday to Friday was for work. In my eyes, Saturday morning was for me, but my family needed me more. God started to deal with me on this. I was on a track to leave my family behind because my actions showed them that other commitments in my life were more important. I knew that I needed to dedicate a day to my family. If they were supposed to be the people I was leading first, then they needed my time and presence more than I needed to play golf. Today, it is rare I commit to anything on a Saturday without it involving my family. I decided that if I needed to play golf, then it would come out of other times in the week, not my family's time. The remarkable result is I don't miss my Saturday morning golf. I have worked my schedule so that I still get my outlet, but it does not come at the sacrifice of my family. This mentality also has seeped into other aspects of my life. There are times when early mornings and evenings require me to be away from home, but now I have become very selective. The world would say that not attending some networking event, client dinner, or staying at the office to get that project done would cost me. I would say that in the kingdom of God, when you have your priorities in alignment, God does not leave you short. One of the best ways to lead your family is to teach them the God-first mentality. This alone has the ability to transform your marriage and home into one of beauty and peace.

In church culture, we tell pastors and church leaders, "Do not sacrifice your kids on the altar of ministry." I would advise business leaders: Do not sacrifice your family in the name of trying to provide financially for your family. Do you have a burden to provide? Yes, but your family deserves your time and presence more than anything else you can provide. When you commit yourself to leading your family before leading your business, favor in your business is around the corner.

A quick word for those who are struggling financially and have to work multiple jobs or long hours just to make ends meet and have limited time to give to their family. Still, make it a priority to create Godly environments in your home. God sees the financial season you are in, and according to His word, He will not leave you. However, if all those extra hours are to fulfill a lavish lifestyle or so little Johny can be in three sports teams at once, then I would challenge you; it is time to make some sacrifices and get back to what really is important, that is, God first!

THE SELF-THIRD MENTALITY

Self-help is a multi-billion-dollar industry. There are more books, podcasts, articles, and resources concerning mind, body, and soul than there have ever been in the history of humanity. The human behavior company Circana works with industry-leading companies to provide consumer data and analytics to give insight into customer buying behaviors and published an article in 2019 entitled, "Self Help Book Sales Are Rising Fast in the US."[2] In this article, they detail how the number of self-help books doubled from 2013 to 2019. The number of accounted-for books with an ISBN in 2013 relating to self-help was 30,897. By 2019, this number had risen to 85,253. In just six years, there had been almost 35,000 books published in just the self-help space. The amazing part about this is it was pre-COVID, the world shutting down pandemic that caused mental health issues to spiral out of control. Our world has seen an epidemic of mental health problems over the last few years, yet there are more and more resources available to help yourself.

What does this tell us about humanity? We need help! We find it very hard to take care of our mind, body, and soul, and the result is that as we deal with more and more self-issues, the generations coming up behind us will deal with them even more. I can say this because while we have more resources than any generation before us has had to deal with body issues, mental issues, and social issues, our generation has more body

---

2   NPD (2020) Self help book sales are rising fast in the US, the NPD Group says, The NPD Group. Available at: https://www.npd.com/news/press-releases/2020/self-help-book-sales-are-rising-fast-in-the-us-the-npd-group-says/ (Accessed: 25 September 2023).

issues, mental issues, and social issues than our fathers, grandfathers, and great-grandfathers generations. The more we learn about how the ingredients of food affect our bodies has not stopped more and more people from becoming obese or suffering heart issues. The more we learn about the dangers of social media, TV, video games, and high screen usage has not stopped us from becoming so dependent on our devices for social and personal interactions. The more we have discovered the importance of stable relationships in a child's life has not stopped a record number of families from becoming divided in divorce. The problem is all the self-help talk. We just cannot help ourselves; we need a higher help!

It is essential to take care of yourself and your own needs. My grandfather died of a heart issue at the age of forty-four in 1954, leaving my father, who was seven at the time, fatherless. I wonder if he lived under the modern medicine of today if my father would have been able to see his father grow old! Life is not guaranteed. We only have one body and one life to make it. If we do not put practices into place to care for ourselves, then life can become challenging, and it may ultimately be very short.

I wish I were better at taking care of my own body. I sometimes get envious of all those early morning gym enthusiasts who have posted the results of their 5-mile run or their extreme cross-fit workout on social media before my alarm even goes off to get out of bed. The struggle is real, and the gym is not a place that I call a friend. However, do not get me wrong, the older I get, the more and more I am becoming aware of my mind, body, and soul. There is no doubt that what you consume affects every facet of your life. Chocolate, caffeine, and alcohol not only have an impact on my midriff, but they also have a massive impact on my mental health. I love chocolate; British chocolate is like no other! If you want to know what heaven tastes like, find a store that sells British goods and get yourself a Galaxy bar, break it, and put a piece of that chocolate on your tongue; you will thank me for it. I also enjoy tea. Yep, I'm that stereotypical British person, and I love coffee. However, I know when I have consumed too much, I start feeling down and depressed. I am becoming more and more aware, and I am making better choices. The taste sensation of much chocolate is not worth the trade-off of being depressed, so I limit my intake.

My grandmother always told her grandkids, "Moderation, everything in moderation." This is so true. This is how God set up this world. We live in a world of balance, a world of variety, and a world where we have everything to live a full and healthy life. When you are not well, you cannot bring your best to those elements you touch, whether that may be your family, your business, or your church. After putting God first and leading your family, before you take care of your business, non-profit, or church ministry, you must ensure you are taken care of. This means putting boundaries in place and setting up guardrails so that you do not get too close to the edge. It means managing your calendar, saying no, probably more than you say yes. It means having a plan for your body, creating space for you, doing something fun, reading books, and developing your skills (not for your job but for your personal development). If you do not take care of your health, your time, and your mind, then the customs of this world will want to try to take care of them for you.

People talk a lot about balance. They say how you need to balance your life between your job, your family, and your other activities. I am going to be honest; I do not believe in balance. In fact, I have a feeling that people who can balance their lives just do not have enough going on in their life to balance. When you feel one area of your life is in balance, it seems another area quickly gets out of balance. There have been times when life has been so busy that I did not know what to do. I remember when we got our first building at our church. It was a leased space that we had to build out. Not having much money, we did much work ourselves instead of contracting it out. I remember being so busy that I was unable to cut my grass for four weeks. You got bit by bugs just walking from the car in the driveway to the front door. Life was impossible to balance. One night, it was dark, and I just had to get it cut. The following day, let me just say the lines in my yard were not straight, but at least it was cut.

I like to use the word rhythm instead of balance. While balance is an impossible task, rhythm can be found quickly, and once you find a rhythm, even the hard tasks seem easier. We all have the same twenty-four hours in a day, yet some people are able to get so much more accomplished in a day. It is not often because they work harder or longer; it is the fact that they have found a rhythm to their day. If you ever go for a run, you will find it is easy to get out of breath pretty quickly. Almost immediately, your body will send signals to your lungs: quit; otherwise, we will not make it. However, if you dig in for a few more minutes, you will get into a rhythm, and once you get into that running rhythm, the body does not hurt as much. When I was pastoring a church and building my insurance business, I found that sometimes the workload and the demands were incredibly great. I look back and wonder how I did it all, but then I remember I had a rhythm to my week. I would use blocks in my calendar. For example, Wednesday was a sermon-writing day. Nothing was allowed to interrupt my day on Wednesday until the sermon draft was finished. There was a rhythm that helped me to get more accomplished. I encourage you to develop a rhythm for your week. A rhythm for your body, your soul, and your mind.

One of my friends, Bob, who is a business coach and exceptional CFO of a manufacturing company, has a daily rhythm he has developed of silent meditation. He will sit down without any distractions in a silent room and close his eyes for thirty minutes to declutter his mind; he said this has totally changed his stress level, and he has been able to develop wise decisions on complex matters just by sitting quietly. I would probably find myself falling asleep if I closed my eyes for 30 minutes. That is somewhat of a joke and partially true. I have developed a new habit or rhythm to my day. I do not do it every day, but a couple of times a week, I will intentionally, in the middle of the day, take a nap! Daniel Pink, in his brilliant book *When: The Scientific Secrets of Perfect Timing*, puts forth the idea of the perfect nap. He calls it a Nappuccino. Pink talks much in his book about your daily schedule and details how we all have an afternoon low point when we are sluggish and unproductive. He tells us to find the afternoon low point, create a peaceful environment, down a cup of coffee (or other caffeinated drink), set a timer for twenty-five minutes, and put our head down to sleep. Typically, it takes the average person 5–7 minutes to fall asleep, giving you 15 to 20 minutes to sleep before the alarm goes off. The caffeine usually kicks in after twenty minutes, so by the time the timer goes off, you are no longer sluggish; you are rested with a spike of caffeine, and you are ready to be productive once more. Trust me, I was skeptical, wondering, like most, it takes me about an hour to get over an hour's nap! This Nappunccino worked! I have been amazed. I am more productive in the afternoons than I have ever been, getting more done than before, even with the extra twenty minutes that I now nap.

The whole point is that if you do not have a mentality that takes care of yourself after you put God and your family first, then you will have very little to give to your business, project, or work you do. The apostle Paul told the church in Corinth, "Do you not know, that your body is a temple of the Holy Spirit within you, whom you have from God? You are not your own, for you were bought with a price. So glorify God in your body" (1 Corinthians 6:19–20, ESV).

Paul was talking about fleeing from sexual immorality, but the lesson here is a more holistic approach to your life. Take care of yourself, your mind, body, and soul. Who you are is so much more important than what you do. When what you do affects who you are, and not in a good way, it is time to stop doing what you do! God is concerned about who you are becoming much more than what you do.

THE BUSINESS-FOURTH MENTALITY

Business is important. A good work ethic is essential. What you do and what you produce is important. Make no mistake, just because we have grace, and I believe that what we do when fully living under grace should not be hard and painful, it does not mean that we shortchange our business, our clients, or our employers. Solomon told those who are lazy to look at the ants. He said,

> *Go to the ant you sluggard; consider its ways and be wise! It has no commander, no overseer or ruler, yet it stores its provisions in summer and gathers its food at harvest. How long will you lie there, you sluggard? When will you get up from your sleep? A little sleep, a little slumber, a little folding of the hands to rest, and poverty will come on you like a thief and scarcity like an armed man.*
>
> — Proverbs 6:6–11 (NIV)

Wow, Solomon did not mince his words. I wonder if he had walked into the bedroom in the middle of the day of his teenage child during summer vacation. Solomon says quit sleeping! Now, obviously, Solomon needed to meet Daniel Pink, and he would have realized that a Nappuccino was a good thing. Solomon isn't referring to a Nappuccino, though; he is talking to those who are sluggish. He tells them the wise understand the seasons and apply themselves to ensure they produce.

In your business or industry, there will be patterns and seasons. Times when you know the workload is a little extra and when there is plenty of breathing room. If you are a tax accountant and want to take a month off in March or April, then do not be surprised if all your clients find another accountant. There is no excuse for laziness, but it is also not just about working harder or longer hours. It is always about working smarter, not harder. I believe the principles in this book, while they may seem foolish to the world's traditions and customs, are principles to be able to work smarter.

The fact of the matter is if you put God first in your life, put your family second, and take care of yourself third, you will be the best you when it comes to your work and your business. When you allow the grace of God to change you and seek His Holy Spirit, then fruit starts to be produced in your life. Galatians 5 tells us that this fruit is love, joy, peace, patience, kindness, faithfulness, gentleness, and self-control. If this fruit becomes evident in your life, you will start to stand out from the rest to your clients, to your employers, and to your peers. You will have times when your values may clash with the world's values, but they will not be able to deny that you are different and that you certainly are not a sluggard.

With the wisdom and power of the Holy Spirit, you will have a wind in your sail when it comes to your work. You will find undeniable peace when the market gets hard, and you will be able to overcome obstacles that most would crumble when faced. When you have a business-fourth mentality, you gain a cheat mode to your work that those who live to put work first will notice and will scratch their heads.

Dan Sullivan, author of *How the Best Get Better*,[3] provides a worktime system that he encourages people to adopt. He explains how the best have preparation days called buffer days, productivity days called focus days, and rejuvenation days called free days. He knows that we need to work smarter and not harder. So we need to plan for days when all we do is preparation and administration. Then, plan for days when

---

3   Sullivan, Dan. *How the Best Get Better.* 2001.

all we do is produce, make, and create. Finally, we need to put days on the calendar when all we do is sharpen the tools in our toolbox: free days. Some do not have the capacity to carve our entire days but could section out hour blocks in a day to do the same. The whole theory behind this is, once again, that word, rhythm. Instead of starting and stopping tasks, when our mind is set to focus on one priority, we are so much more productive. When we give ourselves days to think away from tasks, we become so much more effective. When we take time to work *on* our business instead of *in* our business, the results are astounding.

Many years ago, I heard the story of the tale of two lumberjacks. A young lumberjack was being mentored by an older lumberjack. It was pretty apparent that the old lumberjack was not as physically able as he used to be. One day, the younger lumberjack challenged the older lumberjack to a competition. Whoever could cut down the most trees with an axe in a single day would win. The older lumberjack agreed to the competition. As they began, it was clear that the younger lumberjack had more strength and stamina than his older counterpart. As the younger man gave his all, he would look over to see how the old man was doing; he noticed moments when the older lumberjack was just sitting and taking a break. At the end of the day, the young man boasted that he was the greater lumberjack, so confident of his victory. However, when all the trees were counted, the older lumberjack had significantly cut down more trees than the young man. The young lumberjack was in shock. He could not believe it was possible. He said to the older man, "How is this possible? I worked harder, did not take a break, and sweated more, and you seemed to be sitting down every thirty minutes to take a rest." The older lumberjack replied, "I was not taking a rest; I was sharpening my axe, for you can't cut down many trees with a dull axe!"

This story reminds me of so many people in the marketplace. Work harder, work longer, and put in the sweat equity. The world says if you swing the axe long enough and hard enough, then the tree will come down. Yes, that is true, but what if we spent five minutes sharpening our axe every so once in a while? Imagine how many more trees will fall with less effort and in less time if we sharpen our axe? How are you sharpening your axe? What are you learning? What insight are you gaining? What new skill are you trying to master? What questions are you asking those further along in the journey than you? What Bible scriptures are you reciting? What books are you reading? What podcasts are you listening to?

In September 2021, I handed in my resignation to the owners of my then-insurance agency. It was one of the most difficult decisions and conversations I have ever had to have. I do not like to leave, and I do not really like to say goodbye. It was more difficult because when you work in industries like insurance, when you leave, typically you are asked to leave immediately, rarely there is a notice served, no leaving party, and many times you are not even allowed to say goodbye to your work colleagues, especially when you leave to go to what is seen as a competitor. While this decision was hard, I had prepared myself for it two months prior. I felt stuck and did not know what to do. I had confided in my job predicament to a few close Godly businessmen. The advice I received was exactly what I needed to hear: "Alex, you need to determine in your mind what you are going to do and also what you feel honors God. Once you have made up your mind, go for it; God will make a way."

I left that meeting with my friends, sat in the car, and said to myself, *Right, I'm quitting! God has something better for me. I need to honor God; staying in this job is not honoring. I need to lead my family. What sort of example is this to my family if I stay and compromise my values? I need to show them bold leadership. I need to put myself first before others because if I suffer, how can I serve others? So, I am going to quit and leave it to God.* That was the conversation I had with myself and had determined it in my heart. No less than twenty-four hours later, I sat at my desk and got the most random phone call from someone I had occasionally played golf with. He wanted to ask a question about an upcoming business meeting at the country club we belonged to. Before you knew it, I had told him, without planning to, that I was going to leave my agency. This man owned a smaller insurance agency himself. He confided in me that he was joining forces with a more prominent agency, in which I knew the owners, and they were then going to be part of a larger national corporation. Within three weeks, I had played golf with the owner of the other agency whom I had met on a sales trip to Bermuda years before. I had met the larger corporation and was offered a position almost matching the earnings that I received in my current role. They told me that when they met my wife and me in Bermuda on that trip, their own leadership team had discussed me and said if they ever got the chance to get Alex to work for them, they would jump at it. I had no idea. It is incredible how God can use conversations and connections today that seem totally innocent to set you up to walk in His purposes later in your life.

A few years later, while my life has vastly changed, I have been presented with many great opportunities, yet I still remain with this agency advising people on insurance, making more sales than I ever did before, and have had the doors open to opportunities I could never have dreamt of before. My life is not perfect, and my lifestyle is no Grant Cardone's lifestyle, but when your house is in sync, and the order of your priorities is correct, your business affairs are handled. For if you seek first the kingdom of God and His righteousness, all these other things will be added onto you.

PRAYER FOR ORDER

Father, you require me to seek you first before anything else. Give me the strength to put you above all else. Give me the wisdom to organize my schedule so that those closest to me are not forgotten, and help me to keep the right order in my life so that I honor you, lead my family well, and become the best me possible. Grant me the power to control the urgings of my body so that I stay healthy and have the stamina to give my best every day in all that I do. Help me to prioritize my life in the right order.

CHAPTER 8:
The Manna Mentality

"**L**ARGER ACCOUNTS, THAT IS WHAT I WANT. I'M TIRED OF THE LEVEL of accounts I am selling at, so I will go after larger accounts." That is what I found myself saying after a record year of sales. I had just finished the year with the highest sales revenue, a record for my company and also for myself, and I was incredibly dissatisfied with what I had just accomplished. I was seriously considering my future because the hustle and grind of sales was something I disliked immensely, even though I was successful at it.

Sales leaders, entrepreneurs, CEOs, business owners, revenue officers, and basically anyone responsible for bringing in revenue to a company are rarely satisfied. One sale is not enough; they want two. One record year is a good start, but a decade of consistent growth year over year is what is expected. In the sales world, we call people who bring in the revenue hunters, and hunters are never satisfied with the kill; they always want more.

The sports star who will not stop until they have more championship rings on their finger. The inventor who is not content with one life-changing invention, pursuing more ideas. The franchise owner who believes that they have to open many more stores. The church pastor who has to open more campuses or build bigger buildings. The list could go on and on.

There is something wired in the mind of humanity that tells us that what we have today is not enough; we need more. Is it wrong to have ambition? No, absolutely not. A hunter who has no ambition or drive will not eat. A business leader who does not have a desire to grow will find the world passes them by rather quickly. It was the American writer William S. Burroughs who said, "When you stop growing, you start dying." There is so much truth to this statement, especially in business. However, as Christians, we have to ensure that our ambition for tomorrow does not cloud our contentment for today. Let me explain.

After that record year of sales, I was not satisfied. I wanted more, larger, what I considered better accounts. When you cannot celebrate your successes, not matter how small or great, because you are constantly striving for something better, you will end up becoming very down and depressed. There is joy in stopping and smelling the roses, and if you cannot find the joy and contentment today, then I have news for you that you will not like: you will not find it tomorrow either. When is enough enough? The world will say never. Jesus spoke to this type of worldview through a parable He taught found in Luke 12:

> *And he told them this parable: "The ground of a certain rich man yielded an abundant harvest. He thought to himself, 'What shall I do? I have no place to store my crops.' "Then he said, 'This is what I'll do. I will tear down my barns and build bigger ones,*

and there I will store my surplus grain. And I'll say to myself, "You have plenty of grain laid up for many years. Take life easy; eat, drink, and be merry." But God said to him, 'You fool! This very night, your life will be demanded from you. Then who will get what you have prepared for yourself?' This is how it will be with whoever stores up things for themselves but is not rich toward God.

— Luke 12:16–21 (NIV)

This is a scary parable, especially for those who are responsible for the growth and vision of a company. Wall Street does not like this parable, and neither does the ambition inside of you. We see a man who has it all played out. Work hard, build bigger barns, keep going until you have enough, then rest, relax, and take it easy. This man never got what he wanted because his life was taken before he could enjoy it. This is the story of so many people in our world today. Striving, hustling, hunting for more and more, and never stopping to enjoy the gift that is today. That was me for many years. There were never enough top-caliber clients, there were never enough sales, not enough people in church on Sunday, never enough in the bank account, my golf game was never quite satisfying, and so on. This worldview of relentless ambition can seep into every aspect of your life to the point that you become unhealthy.

My desire is that today, this worldview changes. I am all for vision and going to the next level, but for today, it is time to stop and become thankful for what you have, to delight in what God has provided. When you stop your striving for one moment and give thanks to God for what you have for today, tomorrow does not become such a burden to you. Remember what Jesus said in Matthew 6?

> *So don't worry about tomorrow, for tomorrow will bring its own worries. Today's trouble is enough for today.*
>
> — Matthew 6:34 (NLT)

I believe we can also use the word blessings or the word contentment in the place of worry. Let's try it:

> *So don't worry about tomorrow, for tomorrow will bring its own blessings. Today's blessings are enough for today.*

Or:

> *So don't worry about tomorrow, for tomorrow will bring its own contentment. Today's contentment is enough for today.*

How did that sound? I know when I start to free my mind of the world's striving, there is a freedom and a joy that I find for today. The apostle Paul wrote to the Philippian church:

> *I know how to live on almost nothing or with everything. I have learned the secret of living in every situation, whether with a full stomach or empty,*

with plenty or little. For I can do everything through Christ, who gives me strength.

— Philippians 4:12–13 (NLT)

Paul is teaching us a better way to follow than the world's way. The world will say never be content, strive for more, build and keep building, and never stop. Paul says it does not matter what season you find yourself in. A growing season or a declining season. A bull market or a bear market. A hard market or a soft market. A positive earnings report or a negative earnings report, it doesn't matter; be content in whatever place you are at because your strength comes from the Lord!

This is what I call "the manna mentality." It is a mindset that understands that our provision comes from God, and we should always delight in that provision.

The nation of Israel, which had inhabited and then became slaves in Egypt for over 500 years, had received their freedom. They made a great exodus following the strong and mighty hand of God on display against the nation of Egypt. They had watched as God had delivered them and parted the waters of the Red Sea so they would escape of dry ground. Their enemy had been destroyed, and life should have been good. However, watching God perform the miraculous does not stop the world's methods and customs from swaying your mind away from God.

As Israel had found themselves in the middle of the wildness, the fear and reality came over them that there was not going to be enough food or water for them. So they started to crumble and complain. They complained that God had taken them from security in Egypt to die out in the wilderness.

God heard their grumblings and complaints, and being the gracious and caring God He is, God provided at that moment for them. It was not just that day He provided, but God miraculously provided for the next forty years as the people of Israel wandered about the wilderness.

God had given them a promise. The promise was that He would lead them out of their slavery in Egypt and take them to a land that flowed with milk and honey. God was taking them from a toxic, unhealthy, dangerous culture to a place where they could be fulfilled, safe, and delighted. However, in between these two places, they found themselves in an environment that they did not expect: the wilderness. The place of scarcity, the desert, is a place where many go to die. Following God is not easy, but it does lead you to more extraordinary places and depths you could never have imagined. The problem with following God is that it does require seasons of walking through the wilderness. However, it is in these seasons that God helps to prepare your mind and soul for the promises He desires to pour out on you. It is in the wilderness that God teaches you principles for life that allow the promises of God to be maximized and His purposes fulfilled.

Many have gone through these wilderness experiences in their lives. In fact, if you have never gone through a wilderness experience, watch out because you are probably heading into one, for it is in the wilderness that God shapes and molds us so we can walk into the next season of our life ready for all God as planned. Wilderness experiences are never easy, and some even turn back because they cannot take the thought of living with manna as their only option to survive.

Manna was God's supernatural provision to the people of Israel. As they grumbled about their lack of food, God rained down what is called "manna" from heaven. Exodus 16 tells us what this manna was.

> *Then the Lord said to Moses, "Look, I'm going to rain down food from heaven for you. Each day the people can go out and pick up as much food as they need for that day. I will test them in this to see whether or not they will follow my instructions. On the sixth day, they will gather food, and when they prepare it, there will be twice as much as usual."*
>
> — Exodus 16:4–5 (NLT)

God then rained down food on the people every single day for the next forty years. Talk about a miracle! In a place of no food, Israel had food. They did not have to hunt or strive for it. Each day, they would wake up, and on the ground were the ingredients for food. But there were conditions to this manna. The manna would be provided by God every day, and the people could eat as much as they wanted that day. However, they could not leave some over for tomorrow. If they did leave the food for tomorrow, they would wake up the next day, and the food would be rotten. This was the rule except on the day before the Sabbath. There would be a double portion that day, and they would prepare food for that day and the next day's Sabbath; the food would not be rotten on the Sabbath. On the Sabbath, there would be no manna given. This is precisely what happened, day after day, year after year; God provided for that day. They did not have to worry about tomorrow, for God is a God of today's needs!

Many people, when they think of manna, they think of bread. Many translations of the Bible even say that God rained down bread from heaven, so they think of a loaf of bread on the ground. This is not what manna was. Bread in the Bible means provision and sustenance. Bread meant a daily balanced diet. Even though manna was not bread, they could make bread out of it. Manna was incredible. It was filled with all the nutrients that they needed daily. It was the world's first and best multi-vitamin. Many scholars believe that manna was this grainy, flakey substance that would appear on the ground and could be used to make many foods. Almost like a type of flour, manna was gathered by the people, and then they would make all types of different foods from it. This is just the way that God works. God, while He does the heavy lifting, just requires us to play our part. He is not going to provide miracle after miracle while we just sit down and receive His provision. That would be unhealthy for us, just like a parent does not do everything for a child; no, they provide so the child does not have to worry, but they also expect their child to do their part. Parents of today (myself included) have no problem telling their kids that they have no idea how good they have it. Stories of walking 2 miles to school in the rain and snow, going uphill both ways when "I was a kid" echo car rides to school in the morning. While children of today, for the most part, do not have to go through what their parents went through growing up, children still have to play their part. What they do is never as much as the parents, but they still do something.

This is precisely how God operates. He knows it does not benefit us if He does it all for us. He desires to partner with us. God will do the heavy lifting, but we have a part to play as well. This was exactly God's intention regarding the manna provided in the wilderness. God provided the ingredients, but the people of Israel had to make something with them. In the same way, I believe that God has provided the ingredients for you to be successful and live out purpose in your business or organization. Now, it is up to you to take what God has given and create something beautiful out of it.

It is easy to take what was once awe-inspiring and make it mundane. An exciting adventure can, at times, become a dull ritual if we are not careful. If we are not intentional, it can be easy to view what once brought us life as something that has become tasteless. The incredible romance became a lifeless marriage. The job of a lifetime became a stressful headache. The life-giving church that took away your free time. When we stop to live in the wonder of what God has done in our lives, it does not take long to lose a positive perspective. Without a positive perspective, we stop creating. When we stop creating, we start to live outside the purposes of God, and when we live outside the purposes of God, we start to long for a different type of life. This happened to the Israelites, and if you are not careful, it can happen to you.

> *Then the foreign rabble who were traveling with the Israelites began to crave the good things of Egypt. And the people of Israel also began to complain. "Oh, for some meat!" they exclaimed. "We remember the fish we used to eat for free in Egypt. And we had all*

the cucumbers, melons, leeks, onions, and garlic we wanted. But now our appetites are gone. All we ever see is this manna!

— Numbers 11:4–6 (NLT)

The people of Israel quickly grew tired of the manna! I love Indian food, but I know many people who do not. In 2006, my wife and I were invited to Kolkata in northeast India to preach and sing at a Christmas concert. She did the singing, and I did the preaching. We were there for ten days and stayed on the same road where Mother Theresa lived and did her incredible work. We were given meals, a driver, and a house for ten days. It was a wonderful experience, and there should have been no reason to complain. However, after about six days, I could see my wife having trouble with the food. She said to me, "Everything tastes the same; whether it is breakfast, lunch, or dinner, there is spice I keep on tasting." That spice was coriander. On the last day, we saw a McDonalds. My wife ran to it, only to be disappointed because they don't serve beef in India, and the lamb burger she got, you guessed it, had coriander in it.

It is amazing how too much of a good thing can take away your taste buds. The Israelites started to complain about the manna; they wanted a different taste. They had taken their eyes off the miracle God had provided and instead began to dream of what they used to have. Numbers 11 tells us that it started with the people in the crowd who were not Israelites. There were people who were traveling with them who did not serve God. When people who do not know God walk alongside you, they will receive the overflow of the blessings God is pouring out on you. Do not be surprised that when God rises the tide of your blessings, your boat rises, and other boats around you will rise as well. This was the case for these people who were not Israelites; they were blessed because the people of Israel were blessed. However, notice that it was these people who first complained about the manna. The miracle of the manna was not even for them, but they complained because they craved the food of Egypt. Yes, the same Egypt that enslaved them almost killed them, and gave them very little return on investment for what they received from their incredibly hard work.

People who live according to the world's principles are never satisfied, never content. They are regularly looking at what others have. We have to be careful not to let the people who live by worldly principles cloud our perspective of heavenly principles. I am not saying all the principles of the world are wrong. Some of the world's principles have made many very successful, but when we take our cue from the world, do not be surprised when you start to find complaints about the blessings of God.

The non-Israelites influenced the Israelites. They complained and started to think about the food in Egypt. They blamed God for taking away their appetite. They forgot about the pain of Egypt and just remembered the food. It is easy to be hard on the Israelites when we read their story, but so many of us do this every day. When we live in a world of never enough, do not be surprised when you find yourself wanting bigger and better.

I have a belief that the Israelites got lazy with the manna. Instead of finding new ways to cook and bake it and coming up with new recipes, they got lazy and settled into a rut of just cooking it the same way each day. Instead of thanking God for the provision and then praying for creativity in how to prepare the manna, they complained.

For forty years, the Israelites found themselves living in this situation. Manna after manna after manna. Living with the memory of the leeks of Egypt and hearing of the milk, honey, and grapes of Cannan (the promised land they were traveling to), they forgot to delight in the provision of God for today. I wonder how many of us are living in this moment right now. We are neither here nor there, striving, working, pushing to get to the promised land, tired of the manna for today! The problem is, if we live like the world, they will tell us to keep working harder, push ourselves further, and run over anyone in our way, and then we will get to delight in the promised land, yet for the world, there is no promised land for the world will never be content. They will always want to pull down barns to build bigger barns!

I found myself in this rut not too long ago. I was changing my focus on my business and my ministry, wanting to diversify so I could create more margin in my schedule. This was not a bad desire, and I felt it would honor God in the process. However, when my focus changed, I found that my perspective changed as well. I desired to become more streamlined. I found that my attitude towards my current clients and opportunities was taking a downward turn. These clients who had helped build my business were now becoming an annoyance to me. I had at the beginning of the year written out a list of items I would pray about throughout the year. This is a practice I have done for more than a decade now, and it has been amazing to see how God has answered prayer. One of the items that I wrote on this prayer list was for a certain number of clients who would generate a certain amount of revenue for me. I prayed over this desire with passion for months, believing God would provide. When I did not get the success I had experienced in the past with these clients, I blamed my current clients even more for taking up too much of my time, which I could not spend on acquiring newer, "better" clients. One day, as I sat down to pray through the items on my list before I started my day, suddenly, God spoke to me in that quiet, soul-changing way He loves to do as I got to the prayer about my clients. It wasn't the comforting, let's keep going kind of gentle voice. It was a whisper that said, "You are despising the manna I am giving you, just like the Israelites. Remember how long they traveled in the wilderness because of their complaining!" It hit me! Instead of delighting in the provision of God, I was acting like the rabble in the Israelite camp, dreaming of what I thought was better, forsaking the provision of God before my eyes.

My prayer changed that day, and it has changed every day since. I am no longer praying for bigger, better clients. I know that God will provide them when it is time. My prayer now is this, "Father, I thank you for the manna you are going to provide for me today. May I take that manna and be creative with it? May I learn to use it to its full potential? Father, help me to not only eat this manna but also to delight in this manna. Help me not to think indifferent towards the provision you are giving me today; instead, give me the wisdom to honor you with this manna!"

This has been my daily prayer. When I look at the list of what I am praying through, I still see the better, bigger prayer request, but I now just smile and pray my manna prayer. Let me tell you, since the very first day I prayed this prayer, my perspective has completely changed. I have seen more clients than I ever have had at any point in my career. Not just regular accounts but what the world would call bigger and better accounts. I have seen doors in ministry and the marketplace open like never before. The reason for this is simple: I have found the joy, love, and contentment in the manna that God has rained down every day.

What has God given you today? Who are the staff God has provided you with? Who are the clients God has given? Who are the prospects you have got in front of? Who are the industry leaders that God has opened the door for you to connect with? What materials or resources do you have in front of you? This is manna! It is not to be despised, and it is not to be overlooked. It is manna provided for you to create something incredible. Do not despise it, do not look over it, and do not wish for something better. Delight in it, honor God with it, and watch the miraculous provision of God in your life each and every day.

PRAYER FOR MANNA

Father, I thank you for your provision, which is poured out each and every day. For manna is for my good, to nourish me and sustain me. As I receive what you give unto me, let me not only receive your manna, but let me use it and create something wonderful out of it. As I consume what comes from your manna, let me delight it in, not longing for the leeks of my past life in Egypt or desiring the grapes of my future life in Cannan, but taking in with joy the manna for today.

CHAPTER 9:

The Present Future Mentality

ARE WE THERE YET? THIS IS TAKING FOREVER! THOSE TWO PHRASES are heard regularly on any road trip we take as a family. Whether it be a one-hour journey in the car or a painful sixteen-hour journey, "Are we there yet?" rings from the back seat of our car.

The majority of my wife's family lives in Florida. Living in Maryland, it is a two-hour, often direct flight to Tampa for us to visit. It is an easy plane ride, but there are only so many personal items you can take on the plane. This is why we often make the drive to Florida instead. During the Summertime, my wife and son will often spend an extended time down there, so it is not uncommon for me to drive them down to Florida, fly back home, and then, in three or four weeks, fly back to Florida to drive them home. I do this because I don't want them to have to make the drive alone. However, let me tell you, while the plane ride is a breeze, the car ride is a nightmare.

It normally takes about 15–16 hours, and for long periods, there is nothing to see except the highway in front of you. The older I get, the harder the drive becomes. Children often have a hard concept of timing. As soon as they get a little bored or tired of being in the car, they will often ask, "Are we there yet?"

On this drive to Florida from Maryland, about eight hours in, driving through rural North and South Carolina, I can hear myself saying, "Are we there yet? Are we even close? This is taking longer than I remember?" Knowing that progress is being made, the journey is just not fun!

When we are striving towards a vision, project, goal, or destination, that is so much of our focus. Like a 16-hour car ride, it can at times seem painful, even boring, while we head towards the destination. If you asked anyone on a long car ride, would you rather be at the destination or on the journey? They would tell you the destination. The future always seems more appealing than the present circumstance, for the future is full of hope, so the quicker we can get through the journey to arrive at the destination, the better.

Remember the children of Israel in the wilderness? They began to despise the manna provided and the journey they took in order to get to the promised land. All they wanted was what was promised: a land flowing with milk and honey. However, God knew that it was in the journey that He was molding them and shaping them to become everything He needed them to be when they finally did arrive. God was teaching them to look forward in hope at the future but to pay attention to today, for God didn't just have a purpose for them when they got to the promised land. He had a purpose for them today!

I remember being in my twenties, single, in an entry-level job without an appealing job title, no house to call my own, little money, and little confidence, looking at people in their thirties, wishing I was where they were in life. The people in their thirties were married, had a respectable job title, had bought a house, seemed to have confidence, and were able to buy things. When I got into my thirties, I remember looking at people in their forties, wishing I had what they had. They had children, a nice house, a high-paying job, and lots of confidence; people respected them. Now I am in my forties, it is easy to look at people in their fifties who now have their homes paid off, with their kids either out of the house or old enough to take care of themselves, so now they can organize their schedule without worrying about their kids, their 401(k) is looking healthy, and they seem to have more freedom. I can guarantee that when I get into my fifties, I will be looking at people in their sixties and so on.

There is something within the mind of a human that wants tomorrow to come quicker than tomorrow can or should come. We see the hope of tomorrow and compare it to the journey of today. However, as any wise person will know, walking into tomorrow without having been prepared today will cause problems in the future. There is a reason that the journey today takes time, and sometimes longer than we anticipate, because God is working in and through us today. Tomorrow will not come until today has run its course. The older you get, the more you look back and see all the time that was wasted. If you lose clients, money, relationships, property, businesses, or opportunities, it is hard, but you can always get those back. However, what you cannot get back is time! Time is the most valuable asset you have, and if we are not careful, time can pass us by very quickly.

If you ask an elderly person what they would like more of in life, they will not tell you they want more money, more possessions, more fame, more fortune, more influence, or any of that stuff we think is so important early in our life. What they will tell you is that time is what they want. Back in Chapter 3, we talked about having an abundance mindset. Not to live with a scarcity mindset, but knowing that with God, there is more than enough. That is true for everything except time! There is not an abundance of time. It is often when people reach their sixties that they achieve their greatest accomplishments in life. It is not because they have more strength or energy; yes, they might be more experienced and wiser, but people in their sixties understand that time is in short supply, so it spurs them on to achieve more today, for tomorrow is of no guarantee.

Jesus said in Matthew 6 not to worry about tomorrow, for the worries of today are enough for today. Jesus was not saying not to plan and be ready for tomorrow. He was saying, worry about today first. He was teaching what I call "the present-future mentality."

This is a mindset that is full of hope for tomorrow, dreaming dreams, making plans, casting vision, but it is so connected and present today that they do not miss a beat. In the next chapter, we will talk in more depth about what God desires you to focus on today. For now, though, I want to paint a picture of what a present-future mentality builds their day around.

PRAY FOR WISDOM NOW

It was King Solomon who, when he was asked what he wanted from God, asked for wisdom. Even before he was given divine wisdom, he had enough wisdom to ask for more wisdom. For your business, it is not more capital you need; it is not more market share or better employees; what you need is more wisdom! Look at some of these Proverbs King Solomon wrote about concerning wisdom:

"The fear of the LORD is the beginning of knowledge, but fools despise wisdom and instruction."
— Proverbs 1:7 (NIV)

"Getting wisdom is the wisest thing you can do! And whatever else you do, develop good judgment."
— Proverbs 4:7 (NLT)

"How much better to get wisdom than gold, and good judgment than silver!"
— Proverbs 16:16 (NLT)

"The one who gets wisdom loves life; the one who cherishes understanding will soon prosper."
— Proverbs 19:8 (NIV)

If we are not seeking more wisdom on a daily basis, then we are missing out. Wisdom is the most valuable gift you can give to your business or organization. It does not take the smartest person to understand the value of wisdom. The problem comes from where people try to find wisdom. The world understands the need for wisdom and will seek it. Companies will pay thousands of dollars to hear the wise counsel of a consultant or send their team to hear a business guru speak at a conference. Many seek out Eastern religions to find greater wisdom or try to copy what others are doing to find success.

The problem for many is they fail to understand where wisdom comes from. Solomon was not wise because he was a naturally intelligent guy. Solomon was wise because he received wisdom from the one who gave it, Jehovah, the one who was known as the God of Abraham, Isaac, and Jacob. Solomon wrote, "For the LORD gives wisdom; from his mouth come knowledge and understanding" (Proverbs 2:6, NIV). When you need help, go to the source of all wisdom, that is God.

This has been a daily prayer in our house. It actually started with my wife. She would pray for wisdom consistently, and there would be moments when decisions were made in our house that were so right, yet we knew we were not smart enough to figure it out. I saw a pattern; the more she prayed for wisdom, the better our decisions became, so I adopted this prayer of wisdom of hers. It works; it really works.

In the book of James, we are told to pray for wisdom. Look at what James tells us:

> *"If you need wisdom, ask our generous God, and he will give it to you. He will not rebuke you for asking. But when you ask Him, be sure that your faith is in God alone."*
>
> — James 1:5–6 (NLT)

There are not many times in the Bible that God instructs us that if we pray for a specific thing, He will give it to us without question. Wisdom is guaranteed when you pray to God for it and believe that He is the source of all wisdom. It is like a child who is thirsty. If the child asks their parent for water, a loving parent is always going to give their child a glass of water. Water is needed to sustain life; it is good for you and what your body needs. Now, if the child is thirsty and asks for soda or chocolate milk, then what is the answer? Occasionally, the parent might say yes, but most of the time, they will say no. This is exactly how God operates. He is a loving Father. Wisdom to our soul is like water to our body. He will give it every time. If you ask for that job promotion or that new house, well, that is not guaranteed.

When you think of wisdom for your job, business, or organization like water is to our body, you make sure you pay a daily visit to the well. Praying for wisdom is the most productive act you can do each day. First thing in the morning, before you walk into the office, before you log into your system, before you walk into that meeting, ask God for wisdom for this present moment, not for tomorrow, but for now, and watch how He will give it.

If you think back to bad decisions you made, those deals you should have never struck, those partnerships you should have never entered into, those employees you should not have hired, I am pretty sure they were made without you first praying for wisdom! As Solomon said, "Getting wisdom is the wisest thing you can do!" (Proverbs 4:7, NLT).

ASK GOD TO CREATE CLARITY FOR TODAY

When you live in England, you get used to foggy mornings. The term "London fog" is real. You regularly see overcast skies, but occasionally, those overcast skies turn into a dense fog that blankets the streets. It is quite eerie and unsettling to be outside in a dense fog. You have no clarity of what is in front of you, even if you are familiar with the surroundings. The fog speaks uncertainty into your mind and causes you to second-guess what you know is the right way.

A few years back, I was playing a golf tournament in Delaware. The morning the tournament began, a dense fog laid on the course. You could see about fifty yards in front of you and no more. However, due to the tight schedule of the tournament, there was no opportunity to delay the start until the fog lifted. I remember standing on the first tee, not really knowing where the fairway was. After the direction of one of the local members, I gave myself a start line and made my golf swing. At that moment, I just had to trust that I could hit a straight shot. A few minutes later, to my utter surprise, I found my ball in the middle of the fairway (trust me, that does not always happen, even when the skies are clear!).

When the fog is dense, and you can't see what is ahead of you, then you have to trust in what you have practiced, trust in what you know, and hope that you do not go off course or crash. It takes faith to drive or play golf in the fog. While there are moments in your life and your business when the fog of life falls into a dense cloud, leaving you with the need to carry on in faith, this is no way to live life on a regular basis. If the fog stays around for an extended period, you will eventually find yourself going off course or crashing, no matter how much confidence or talent you have. You need clarity to be able to move forward. Clarity in your mind, clarity in your soul, clarity in your vision, and clarity in your strategic decisions. While the world will either freeze due to indecisiveness or be reckless and move forward without direction, for the follower of Jesus, there is no reason why you cannot have the clearest clarity even in the densest fog. If you are praying for wisdom and living a life that honors God, He will direct you.

In fact, the Bible speaks to this. In Psalm 119:105, we are told that God's Word is a lamp for my feet and a light to my path. This means when what is ahead of us is a dark, dense fog with little sign of direction, when we open up the Word of God (remember the right order mentality of putting God first and His Word first), then when everyone else is walking forward blindly, you as a Christ-following business leader are walking through a lit up path of clarity.

I love the promise that God spoke through the Prophet Isaiah. "See, I am doing a new thing! Now it springs up; do you not perceive it? I am making a way in the wilderness and streams in the wasteland (desert)"[4] (Isaiah 43:19, NIV). God does not always cause the entire fog to lift. The skies are not always crystal clear, but what He promises is that He will make a way for you to clearly walk forward in the midst of a place where others are lost. He will light up a path for you to walk through, so one day, you will arrive at your metaphoric golf ball and find it exactly in the middle of the fairway of your life, exactly where it is supposed to be.

While the world is hacking it in the rough, trying to advance their ball towards their goal, you are living in the clarity and faith that God is lighting up the path with your ball in the short grass. This is why, after you pray for wisdom, you seek clarity. Clarity for today, then clarity for tomorrow, next week, next month, six months from now, next year. You may already have your agenda or to-do list for today, but before you get started, seek the Word of God and receive the clarity that comes from seeking Him.

---

[4] Word in parentheses added by the author.

The whole reason you need clarity for today is that God has a purpose, not just for tomorrow, but God has a purpose for you today, and when you have clarity, it is easy to see what God is doing even in the mundane tasks of today. You don't want to miss what God is doing today, because if you miss it today, you are very likely to miss it tomorrow as well. I have a prayer that I present before God every day before I begin my day: "God, give me wisdom for today; allow me the clarity of what I need to do and where I need to go for today so that tomorrow, next week, and next month will be a little clearer, in order that my life honors you in all I do, say and think."

REVELATION FOR TOMORROW

If you are like most effective leaders, then you are someone who is forward-thinking. You are probably thinking ahead of where you are at, out in front, paving a way for your people or organization to follow. I often see the business leader as having two roles. If your business is a line of people making their way through the jungle, then the leader firstly is walking at the back, shouting out motivating words, celebrating the steps their people make in front of them, acting as the safety net and protection so that the people at the end do not get lost or snatched by a predator. However, I also see the role of the leader as the one out front, further along than everyone else, with a machete in hand, carving out a path for their people to follow.

The goal of this book is not to go into detail concerning the individual tasks and methods that you as a leader must take to succeed. The intention is for you to seek the wisdom of God, when you do, then you will know the details of how to be the best leader you can be in the corporate jungle you currently find yourself in. I do want to touch on how you need to think about tomorrow. For much of this book, we talk about trusting in God for today because God has a purpose for today. It is important to know that future thinking is a Godly act. Dreaming of a hopeful tomorrow is a theme consistent throughout the Bible. Prophecy is a main element of Scripture; terms like "blessed hope," "heaven," and the "return of Jesus" speak to tomorrow's world. Without a vision and a glance toward tomorrow as a leader, you will find yourself often left behind in a market that never stops. The likes of Sears, Kodac, Blockbuster, and many other companies that were once so prominent in the marketplace are either no more or not even serious players in their industry because they failed to see past the success of today into the unknown of tomorrow.

Solomon once again said, "Where there is no vision, the people are unrestrained, But happy is one who keeps the Law" (Proverbs 29:18, NASB). It is a vision that keeps the people focused and moving forward. Without a compelling vision, then your people will create their own vision. When you stop communicating, they start communicating with each other. If you do not set the agenda or plan for the future, your people will take the future into their own hands. This is why Solomon says that when there is no vision, people cast off restraint. Many Bible translations use the word revelation instead of vision. Revelation is a good word to use because it distinguishes the difference between how the world thinks and how the Christ follower thinks.

The world will say, dream it, build it, and in the words of the movie *Field of Dreams*, they will come. For those who put their trust in God and follow godly wisdom, they know that this is not always the case. When we follow our own dreams and visions without God, then the results are in our hands. We have to work at it, find a way, create a pathway, and carve a roadway to fulfill that vision. The percentages of completion of the dream are not good. When you seek the revelation of God and God's vision, then what is required is obedience to God's leading. He is the one who creates a roadway in the wilderness. He is the one who works hard to carve out a path for you to walk through.

The word revelation may scare some people. They think of the book of Revelation or some old prophet saying, "Thus says the Lord." However, when you think of revelation, think of a download. If you need to transfer a file from the cyber cloud onto your computer, you need to download it. What is required is the available download, an internet connection, a computer able to receive the download, and a human that gives the computer the command to download. God's revelation is just like this. His revelation is the file, the Holy Spirit is the connection, and your life and your person are the computer, and your mindset and willingness to hear from God is the human command to say download!

It is known that it takes two to tango; well, it also takes two to receive revelation, God and you! Both have to play their part. God never fails. He is always doing His part; the stumbling block is often our willingness to hear from God. If you need a vision for tomorrow, then what you really need is a revelation from God. It's time to hit the download button and receive.

You may be thinking, "This sounds easier than it actually is." When you commit to putting your own feelings, desires, wants, and needs to the side and present your life as a living sacrifice, as Romans 12 puts it, be intentional about asking for revelation and then taking time to be still and listen to the Holy Spirit. You will be amazed at how much fresh vision you will receive. What's more, His vision is always greater than your vision. You will look back at your dreams and realize they were far too small.

Part of my morning prayer life involves a prayer for revelation. It goes something like this, "Father, let me hear your voice above the noise, fill me today with your Holy Spirit and pour out fresh revelation on me. As you pour, allow me the humility and sensitivity to hear what you have to say. Then, give me the strength and the boldness to follow where you lead."

I challenge you to try this for a few weeks. You will be surprised at the clarity and vision you have for your business and company through the process.

PRAYER FOR TODAY AND TOMORROW

Father, thank you for the gift that is today. As I go about my day, allow me to see what you are doing in the moment. Give me the vision for not only what path I will take tomorrow but give me the vision to see how you are working today. Help me to be present in the moment, to not want to rush through today, but to take the time and look around to see you at work in my life. I know the path I walk today will set me up for greater walks tomorrow, so provide me with the patience and awareness to understand the present that is today.

CHAPTER 10:
The Divine Encounter Mentality

HAVE YOU EVER EXPERIENCED A UNIQUE SITUATION THAT JUST DID not seem normal and got you wondering if it was just a coincidence or not? Are coincidences really just coincidences? Before we get all philosophical, I will answer that question. Yes, there are moments that are just a coincidence. It just happens that you see something you were talking about earlier in the day, or you bump into someone who supports the same sports team as you in a city where everyone else supports another team. There is no mystery to happenings like these. However, there are moments when what you fall into is more than just a coincidence.

When you purchased your car, you probably thought that it was very unique. Not many people drove the car you bought, and only a limited amount of people had the color or trim package you chose. Yet, the moment you drove that car off of the lot of the car dealer, something amazing happened; suddenly, everyone else purchased the same car as you as you saw it on the road everywhere! Have you ever felt like that? If you have, then you are not alone. This type of feeling or sensation is called the Baader-Meinhof phenomenon or, as some call it, Frequency Illusion.

A man named Terry Mullan was talking to his friend one day about a notorious West German gang called the Baader-Meinhof gang. They were a left-wing terrorist gang from Germany. The very next day, Terry Mullan saw a newspaper article about this gang, decades after they became no more. What are the chances of that? This incident appeared in a letter to a newspaper in Minnesota in 1994, and it became known as the Baader-Meinhof phenomenon. The premise is that either a word, phrase, item, or idea that you have been thinking about seems to appear more frequently in your environment. The amazing part about this frequency bias is that you believe deep down that it did not happen before you notice it.

This is why you believe you are the reason that everyone bought the same car as you, or you are a fashion setter because the moment you purchased those new shoes, everyone else started to wear them. I am going to burst your bubble! You are not the trendsetter you think you are; it is frequency bias going on. The Baader-Meinhof phenomenon says that once you see something, your mind is awakened to the reality of what you have seen, and then you start to see it everywhere. It is not that what you now see was not there before; it is now you are aware of it.

There is a similarity between this frequency bias and the Holy Spirit. The apostle Paul, writing to the church at Ephesus, said,

> *Once you were dead because of your disobedience and your many sins. You use to live in sin, just like the rest of the world, obeying the devil – the commander of the powers in the unseen world. He is the spirit at*

> *work in the hearts of those who refuse to obey God. All of us used to live that way, following the passionate desires and inclinations of our sinful nature. By our very nature, we were subject to God's anger, just like everyone else. But God is so rich in mercy, and he loved us so much, that even though we were dead because of our sins, he gave us life when he raised Christ from the dead, (It is only by grace you have been saved!) For he raised us from the dead along with Christ and seated us with him in heavenly realms because we are united with Christ.*
>
> — Ephesians 2:1–6 (NLT)

There is so much that can be unpacked out of Paul's words. Thinking back to the grace mentality, remember, it is all because of Christ! However, I want to focus on what Paul said that you once were and now what Paul says you are. You were dead! Now you are alive! This is Christianity 101. We were dead because of our sins; now, we have been made alive with Christ because of Christ! Paul is speaking about our spiritual nature and our soul, but this resurrection from the spiritual death that God brings us through does not just apply to a moment when we come back to God and ask God to save us and make us new. No, this new life now runs through every ember and fiber of our being. What now should happen is a frequency bias towards the movements and workings of God.

When you were dead in your sins, it would have been impossible to notice God. When you are spiritually dead, it is impossible to see what is spiritually alive. You did not notice the people God brought into your life. You did not see the hand of God working on your behalf. You did not feel the workings of the Holy Spirit close to you as God was making a way for you to come to Him. Yet, after you find Christ, suddenly, your whole being is awakened, and you see life everywhere. You start to see God in creation, you see Him working in your family, you see Him meeting your needs, and you see what you once thought was a coincidence is now the hand of God at work. Your mind has been awakened to the Holy Spirit, and you see Him everywhere!

God is working in your business right now. There is a divine encounter you can have today, amongst the meetings, the video calls, the administrative tasks, or that vision planning session. These are not just regular tasks or meetings; these are environments where God is in the middle.

When we planted our church in 2010, the process began about a year before. We did not have a large launch team or the backing of a larger church. It was a grassroots organization when, at times, it felt like the grass was larger than the small group we had gathered! I had just come out of several years of vocational church ministry, serving as a staff pastor in a number of roles. The church we had just come off of staff from had been hard work. It was a church that had been through a tough time; they had lost many of their members through some shady dealings from a former treasurer, and they were in pain. We knew the Senior Pastor from the former church we had been on staff at out in Missouri, and he invited us to come. Still, to this day, I find it amazing that we actually took on these roles. It was certainly a God moment because the church was not my style, nor did we feel up to the task of helping rebuild a dying church. However, through the grace and power of God, that church did survive and not only survived, but it started to thrive.

For all the growth the church started to experience, there was a problem. The staff members were expected to work, work hard, and basically not go home until everything got accomplished. Looking back, our leadership was not strong enough to understand the need to raise up leaders. We were often told that we were paid by the church to do the church work and that it was a privilege to work at a church. Let me say that just because it is a church, it is not immune to an unhealthy culture or bad leadership. This is what we began to experience. Sixty to seventy-hour work weeks were not uncommon. Eating take-out most days because we had so much work caused our bodies to inflate to unhealthy proportions. However, what I felt more than anything during those years was a distance between the world and our lives. I did not like it. This distance was not a healthy one, for the gap that appeared was in our friends and relationships. One day, I sat in my church office feeling that I was going to go crazy in my church bubble, coming to the understanding that I had no opportunities to tell people far away from God about Jesus because I was consistently around Christians and the hours we were working did not allow me to find a hobby where people who were far away from God were. This was a real problem and is still a huge problem in many churches today. If pastors and staff are not modeling what it is like to be the ambassadors of Jesus to a lost, broken, and dying world, then how would we ever expect the members of our churches to do the same?

It was out of that season that we planted a church. However, with now not having any non-believing friends, we had to start the process of integrating back into what I called "normal life." My wife and I began to pray for divine encounters and divine appointments. Wherever we would go, to the people we would meet, we prayed this simple prayer, "God, let there be a divine appointment today where people can experience a divine encounter with you." The more we prayed, the more our prayers were answered. We started to notice God in the middle of all that we did. From the secular jobs we both got to conversations with our neighbors to people we would talk to randomly around our suburban town. Suddenly, we were walking into divine appointments on a regular basis, which God was using so people could have a divine encounter.

It is not that these people were not available before, and it was not because God was not setting up these God moments; it was just our minds were almost dead to the fact that God wanted to use us to reach out to others far from Him. Once our minds were awakened to the fact that God was moving and He wanted to use me to speak to others, suddenly it was like that new car; I saw it everywhere I went.

That is a prayer our family still regularly prays. "Lord, give us a divine appointment today so that someone can experience a divine encounter with you." The other day it was the last day of the summer vacation for my son before he went back to school for the year. I stepped out of my office a few hours earlier to spend some time as a family. We gave him the choice of where he wanted to go, and his choice was to go shopping. He obviously had his mind on some new sneakers and thought this was his perfect opportunity. I had a meeting later that night at church for a committee I was serving on. As the day fell into early evening, I knew I had to leave, so we sat down at the wonderful little farm store that had turned more into a deli. There were a few tables we could have sat at, but we chose a high-top table nearer the back of the deli. Within the space of 30 minutes, I was having a conversation with a couple at the table next to us about church and God. My wife and son had gone to the bathroom, and I had struck up the conversation. This is not me; I would rather sit by myself in silence than try to start a conversation with a stranger. That is Raquel, my wife's giftedness. We discovered that we had so much in common. They were building a home near where we lived and had been through some really tough church experiences. I won't bore you with the details, but as we walked back to our car that night, my wife turned to me and said, "That was a God moment; He certainly set up a divine appointment there." Then she asked me, "How did the conversation start?" I had no clue; all I knew was that God was in the midst. I failed to make it to my church committee meeting that night, initially feeling guilty, then realizing, no, this was a God moment; he wanted me in that deli that night, not in a church meeting room.

 The amazing thing about this night was that the next day, the gentleman texted me, saying how he and his wife had talked about how meeting us was not a coincidence; it was a God-moment!

 There are God-moments given to us each and every day. God is an appointment setter. He is setting up divine appointments for you to attend, for He desires to use you so that other people can have divine encounters with Him. God has got you in that company for a reason. You met that colleague or that person of influence for a purpose. You had that conversation with the stranger or got your plans changed because God is working and moving in your life. The more you become aware of the divine nature that God moves in your life, the more you will see it. The more you see it, the more you will become amazed by it.

I love to set goals—sales goals, physical goals, and giving goals. I even have a goal for the number of books I want to read in a year. However, I have discovered that in life, and especially when it comes to my work, Jesus encounters triumphs over goals that are met every single time. I can crush past a monthly goal, and it feels good, but there is no feeling like there is when you walk out of an interaction with someone knowing that you helped someone have a Jesus encounter.

What if we changed the expectations? Instead of seeking to hit our next quarterly goal, we set a new goal, the divine encounter goal. How many divine appointments can we identify and allow God to use us to those He is placing before us? Once you open your eyes to the movements of God, you will see God's divine encounters everywhere.

PRAYER FOR DIVINE APPOINTMENTS

Father, I know you are working and have a desire to use me. Here I am, open and willing to be used by you. Help me to open my eyes to see how you are working and moving today. I pray for a divine appointment today where I can be used so that someone else can have a Jesus encounter! Help me not to miss how you want to work in the lives of the people I meet. Give me a frequency bias to your movements and workings.

CHAPTER 11:
The Generous Mentality

THERE IS NO DENYING THE POSITIVE EFFECTS ON SOMEONE'S LIFE when they choose to be generous. Just performing a simple good deed creates a feeling of accomplishment. Time magazine published an article entitled "Being Generous Really Does Make You Happier."[5] This article referenced a study by researchers from the University of Zurich in Switzerland that told fifty people they'd be receiving $100 over a few weeks. They were split into two groups. The first group was instructed to spend the money on themselves, and the second group was instructed to spend the money on someone else they knew.

The researchers started by asking both groups to think about a friend they would like to give a gift to and how much they would spend if they could on that person. The researchers took MRI scans to measure activity in three areas of the brain associated with social behavior, generosity, happiness, and decision-making.

---

5   MacMillan, A. (no date) Happiness: Being Generous Makes You Feel Better, Time Magazine. Available at: https://time.com/collection/guide-to-happiness/4857777/generosity-happiness-brain/ (Accessed: 26 September 2023).

As the groups thought of the people they would like to give a gift to, their response and also the activity in their brain through the MRI showed a distinction between the two groups. The group who were to give their $100 away, on average, made more generous decisions throughout the study, while those who were tasked with spending money on themselves made less generous decisions. The MRI also showed for group two (the giveaway $100 group) that there was more interaction between the parts of the brain levels of happiness, and physically agreed they felt greater happiness after the experience.

Time magazine went on to say that the happiness levels from giving are not dependent on how much a person gives; it is from the actual act of being generous to others. They reported that even in older people, health and life expectancy greatly improved the more generous a person was.

This is a principle the world gets, but many Christ followers still have not figured it out. The more generous you are, the more benefits you receive in return. Whether that be greater resources, better health, or just a happier feeling as you go about your day. I have watched and spoken to many the world would call successful people, people who have achieved much, become wealthy, or have gained incredible influence, and I would say one of the greatest differences between people who achieve this type of success and people who seem they are on the hampster wheel of trying to produce success is generosity. It is not because successful people are more intelligent. It is not because they have had a market advantage or been in the right place at the right time. It is because they have been generous.

I think of some of the successful people I have worked for over the others; they were all incredibly generous. Then I think about some of the ones who were less successful; most of them were a little stingy.

Before we go any further, I want to clarify that I do not believe that if you give, you will automatically be blessed with success and fortune. When you give to get back, then you are giving out of the wrong motives. This formula does not and will not work for you if you give out of the wrong motives. In the business world, you see this happen all the time. There are often wrong intentions or a catch behind someone's surface generosity. Be careful of people who seem to be generous in one moment but withhold from others in another area. If the CEO is being generous to their executive team, but the workers on the shop floor can barely make ends meet, there is an issue.

Those who are generous by nature have discovered in life that you do not hold on to temporary things too tightly. They have an open hand instead of a closed fist. When your hand is open to others, yes, you may give away what you have, but then your hand is open to receiving more. You cannot receive when your fists are closed or you are holding onto what you have too tightly. People who are genuinely generous are people that others want to be around, not because they give stuff away but because they are a joy to be around. They are happier, kinder, and less pretentious.

For a Christ follower, it is even more important to show a spirit of generosity. The Bible tells us that we are not our own; we are bought with a price (1 Corinthians 6:19–20). All we have is the Lord's, so why should we hold on to what we have? It is not ours in the first place. We see verse after verse in the Psalms and Proverbs that speaks to giving to the poor and needy, and you will receive back. It is a biblical principle that when you are generous, you will receive back. Even Jesus said, "Give, and it will be given to you. A good measure, pressed down, shaken together, and running over, will be poured into your lap. For with the measure you use, it will be measured to you" (Luke 6:38, NIV).

Jesus is the one who tells us that when we give, it will be given back. The level of blessing you receive is based on the measure you are willing to pour out on others. However, we have to remember that this is not a give-to-get-back principle. It is giving with the right heart, spirit, and attitude. There is a disturbing story in the Bible of a married couple who gave out of the wrong motives. The story is found in Acts 5. Their names are Ananias and Sapphira. This is their story:

> *Now a man named Ananias, together with his wife Sapphira, also sold a piece of property. With his wife's full knowledge he kept back part of the money for himself, but brought the rest and put it at the apostles' feet. Then Peter said, "Ananias, how is it that Satan has so filled your heart that you have lied to the Holy Spirit and have kept for yourself some of the money you received for the land? Didn't it belong to you before it was sold? And after it was sold, wasn't the money at your disposal? What made you think of doing such a thing? You have not lied just to human beings but to God." When Ananias heard this, he fell down and died. And great fear seized all who heard what had happened. Then some young men came forward, wrapped up his body, and carried him out and buried him. About three hours later his wife came*

in, not knowing what had happened. Peter asked her, "Tell me, is this the price you and Ananias got for the land?" "Yes," she said, "that is the price." Peter said to her, "How could you conspire to test the Spirit of the Lord? Listen! The feet of the men who buried your husband are at the door, and they will carry you out also." At that moment she fell down at his feet and died. Then the young men came in and, finding her dead, carried her out and buried her beside her husband. Great fear seized the whole church and all who heard about these events.

— Acts 5:1–11 (NIV)

This couple wanted to show a spirit of generosity, but they had the wrong heart. They told the church in Jerusalem that they gave all they had received from selling a field, but they lied. They wanted to seem more generous than they were. The issue for Ananias and Sapphira was that they lived their lives close-fisted instead of open-handed, and it caused them to have wrong motives, which eventually led to their death. I wonder how many times we like to show the perception that we are generous people, but on the inside, we really want to keep it all for ourselves.

I am a dessert person. Bring out the dessert tray, and you have won my heart. While I love my family dearly, if I order a dessert on the menu and it is beyond exceptional, I do not want to share it. I will say the proper statement after receiving the dessert, "Does anyone want to try it?" I am just fine with someone trying it, but don't take more than a bite, and make sure it is not a big bite at that. When there is something you want to hold onto and consume for yourself, it is very hard to give it away. I am learning that it is going to turn out right if you share your dessert, and in time, I know I will discover the joy of giving my dessert away! However, the lesson here is that if the world has figured out how important generosity is, then as ambassadors for Christ, how much more generous should we be? The answer is that we should be leading the way in living out a spirit of generosity.

There are four ways that you can live out a life of generosity. It does not matter what your personal net worth is, how much margin you have in your life, or what your personality is; we can all embrace a genuine spirit of generosity.

TIME

We have spoken on many occasions throughout this book about time, and here we are again. For the business leader, managing a complex schedule, devoting their presence to their family, and also being a contributing member of their church, time is probably what you lack the most. It is important to protect your time, for unless you protect your time, then no one else will. Get into a habit of saying no more than yes, and you will find it will bring you so much more margin in your life, which in turn helps keep stress at a minimum and your health in check.

This is why time is one of your most precious possessions because there is so little of it. However, in order to live with a generous mentality and to be truly known as a generous person, we cannot hold onto those items that we long to keep. Time is something to be protected but also to be given away. When you choose to take what is most valuable to you and use it to help others, there is something very powerful that occurs! In the area of time, I am a believer that the more you give away, the more you will receive in return. Now, for the mathematicians amongst us, this makes no sense. Time is limited to twenty-four hours a day. It is impossible to get time back when you spend it. Yes, you are correct. To my knowledge, time has only stood still twice in history, one time to Joshua, the leader of Israel, and the other time to King Hezekiah, both documented in the Old Testament. The chance of time standing still for you is pretty much zero!

When I say you will get time back, I am not referring to the hands on a clock going back or you receiving more hours in the day. When you give your time to others in need, then I believe that God rewards you for that, and you receive time from others you would not believe you could receive. Let me show you a few possible examples. When you, as a salesperson, give your time generously to the new guy on the team, you get into that account you have been working at quicker than it normally takes to get a meeting. When you, as a project leader, take time to help another department strategize over their project, your project runs smoothly with no delay. When you, as a consultant, spend time helping someone starting out in the industry, one of your heroes gives you the time to pick their brains!

There is no scientific evidence for this, there is no math formula, and there is no university study into human behavior, but it happens time after time, day after day, in coffee shops, board rooms, offices, and restaurants all over the world. God rewards those who are generous with their time. The measure you pour out is the measure you receive.

Who can you give of your time to today? Not to benefit you but to benefit them. You know that blessings will come from it, but something even greater happens when you allow yourself to be generous with your time. It allows God to work in and through you, and maybe today is the day someone has a Jesus encounter because you decided to be generous with your time!

RESOURCES

When people think about being generous, they think about money, particularly giving money. Yes, money is part of being generous, and we will talk about how money plays into the Christian leader's mindset in the next chapter, but money is only a small part of being a person of generosity. There are very wealthy people who give a lot of money away to others, and while it seems generous to them, what they give is not even a dent for them financially. Would you call them generous if they are giving a small part of their surplus? Then you have some people who may give what seems very little value, but for them, it comes at a huge cost. Who is more generous, the one who gives a lot out of their surplus or the one who gives a little, but it costs them a lot? There is an illustration in the Bible that Jesus uses to teach His disciples about this thought. In Luke 21, Jesus sees many rich people putting their money into the offering box. The clatter of many coins into the box rang through the temple. Then, a poor widow drops two small coins in the box. Everyone knew how much the widow had given, which was not much compared to the rich people. However, Jesus instructs His disciples that the widow, in fact, gave more; this was because she gave out of her poverty, and the others gave out of their surplus. Jesus is looking for people who can give sacrificially, not just out of a surplus.

Money is not the only way someone can be generous, though. You have other resources in addition to money that can be used for the benefit of others. The parable of the talents is an incredible yet chilling example of what Christ's followers should do to steward the resources they have been given. The story, once again told by Jesus in Matthew 25, gives the account of a master who left to go on a long journey and left some of his resources to his servants to look after. One servant received five talents, one servant two talents, and the third servant received one talent. When the master returned, he found that the servant with five talents had turned the five into ten. The servant with two talents had turned the two into four, but the servant with one talent had been so scared to lose what had been given to him that he hid the talent and did nothing with it. The master rebuked the third servant, took his talent, and gave it to the one with five talents. Jesus is teaching us that we have all been given resources. If we live with a closed fist, scared to lose what we have, then we are not living in the purpose that resource that was given to us. We are to use the resources we have been given for the purposes of God; as we use them, do not be surprised if God multiplies them. What resources do you have that you can use for God's purposes? What do you have that you have held so tight, fearing you will lose it?

The Christ follower is a steward of their resources. The world will tell you that what you have is yours, you earned it, and you get to do with it as you wish. However, this is a lie! What you have is not yours; it is all a gift from God. He is the owner, and you are the manager. You are to manage your resources to the owner's (God's) expectations. I love what my friend, Pastor Josh Finley, says, "Your bread is to eat, and your seed is to sow; make sure you don't eat your seed and sow your bread." The resources you have are your seed. When you sow them for the sake of others in acts of generosity, you will reap a harvest. Make sure you sow your resources; don't eat them!

What are the resources you have? Your finances, your property, your giftedness, your education, your manpower, your food, your skills, I could go on. What you have in your hand is a resource; don't keep it for yourself; sow it and watch what God can do with what is in your hand!

WORDS

I am a words-of-affirmation person. If you say nice words to me and tell me how great I am, then I am not only flattered, but I am motivated to do more. Your words have power, and how you use your words has an incredible effect on those close to you. Words have the ability to lift someone up, but they also have the power to pull someone down. The old saying says, "Sticks and stones may break my bones, but words will not hurt me." It sounds good, but it is false. Words can hurt more than a stick or a stone. It is easy to heal from a stick; it can take years of therapy to recover from a word that was harshly spoken.

It was with words that God spoke the world into being. Jesus in the Gospel of John is referred to as the Word. Your words have the ability to bring into existence what was not there before. Make sure that you are bringing in words that edify people towards God, not words that leave people discouraged. The apostle Paul to the Ephesians wrote:

> *"Let no corrupting talk come out of your mouths, but only such as is good for building up, as fits the occasion, that it may give grace to those who hear."*
>
> — Ephesians 4:29 (ESV)

If we are ambassadors of Christ, we are representing Christ wherever we go. This means the words we speak to others are a reflection of the Christ in us. Many of us have to try very hard to hold our tongue. The book of James refers to it as a fire, with the power to control our whole body like a rudder controls a ship. Out of your mouth can come sweet and bitter. Make sure that your words are sweet.

When I was in sixth grade, our English Literature teacher had each class member read out loud in front of the class one by one. Some of the kids in my class were great readers, and some were not. My teacher, whose name was Mrs. Smith, would acknowledge those who read well and stay silent with those who did not read as comfortably. Then, it came my turn. Back in sixth grade, I was incredibly shy. The thought of reading in front of a class caused me to panic greatly. I felt my sweaty hands cause the book to almost slip out of my hand. As I started to read, the words on the page appeared all jumbled. I read for about two minutes when Mrs. Smith stopped me. She declared to the class that she had just heard the worst piece of reading she had ever heard by a sixth grader and indicated to the next reader to begin. Not only did I feel incredibly embarrassed, but those words started to define me. Unless I had to for a school assignment, I did not pick up a book for almost ten years after that day. I had decided in my heart that I was a bad reader and would never embarrass myself again. When I became a pastor, the thought of reading my Bible in public brought back all those memories from sixth grade. One day, through a time of worship, I heard the quiet voice of God say, "Mrs. Smith's words do not define you; my words do. I have called you to preach. I will give you the words, and reading will not be a problem again." This was such a defining moment in my life. Never again have I had an issue reading in public. That day, I found the joy and incredible benefit of reading books.

You have a choice: to be generous with your words, to say whatever you feel should come out of your mouth, or to stay silent and say nothing. Some people have no filter and tear others down, but most listen to their mother's advice when she says, "If you have nothing good to say, then don't say anything at all." I would like to challenge you and say that neither of these two choices is what you should do. Silence can be as painful to someone as words that put them down. The choice in whatever environment you find yourself in should be to choose to be generous with your words. Whether you have to be straight, honest, or rebuke someone, you can still be generous with your words. Proverbs 16:24 (NLT) says, "Kind words are like honey— sweet to the soul and healthy for the body."

The business world is full of choice words. Just sit in a business meeting for a few moments, and you will soon realize that there is very little thought amongst most about the words that come out of their mouths. Many have no regard for the feelings of others. Imagine the impact you can have on the lives of the people you interact with on a daily basis if you make the choice to control your tongue and become more generous than ever with your words. Bring the honey to your next conversation; let kind words be abundant.

INFLUENCE

The fourth way you can have a generous mentality is by being intentional to be generous with the influence you have achieved. Each one of us has influence at our disposal. There is an influence we can lean on when we need help. So many business people work hard to develop influence with others. It was Dale Carnegie who wrote the classic *How to Win Friends and Influence People*. There is a deep desire among so many to be a person of influence. We even have people who pursue a career through social media to become an influencer. Influence is not something you can buy; it typically comes at a cost, and that cost is through cultivating relationships. However, most people try to gain influence for their own development and purposes. Some work at it to become famous, others do it to open doors to greater opportunities.

Whether your influence is over your family, your friends, the people in your church, your team at work, your entire staff, or you are an influential figure in your industry, the influence you have can be used for just your own purposes or ambition. What if you used your influence to help others?

One day, ten lepers came to Jesus to ask for healing. Jesus had influence over sickness and had the power to restore health to these lepers. Jesus did not ask them what was in it for him. He went ahead and used the power he had to heal the lepers. All ten went away healed, but only one came back to thank him. If that had been me, I probably would have put a condition in a contract before I healed them, stating that they were legally bound to come back to thank me. It is a good job Jesus does not follow my advice; if so, then only one person would have found healing that day. Jesus used His influence over sickness to heal, even though He did not get anything in return except one thank you.

Back in the 1990s, my Father pastored a church in the Dudley area of England. The church at the time was a small to medium-sized church that had been board-run without a pastor for many years. When my father was hired, it appeared there was a power struggle. The board had gotten used to calling all the shots and leading the vision and direction of the church. When my father tried to assume the role that the lead pastor should, relations with some of the board members took a downward turn. It got to a point where some of the board members had decided that they wanted to fire my father. Without his knowledge, they had written a letter and sent it out to the entire congregation, calling for a special meeting to have a vote of no-confidence in the pastor. The church is full of human beings, and anything with human influence will eventually go through ugly times. This was ugly, but I'm glad Christ's love for us is not dependent on us being pretty; even in our ugliest moments, He still loves us! The vote of no-confidence did not go as planned for the board. The church voted overwhelmingly in confidence for my father. Some of the board members had egg on their faces, and some resigned, eventually leaving the church. However, one of the board members, who happened to actually be one of my best friend's dad, who had joined in the revolt, had found himself in hot water. He was an outside sales representative for a technology company, and his job depended on him being on the road. Through months of road travel, he had racked up twelve points on his driver's license and was summoned to court to have his license officially suspended. Without his license, he would lose his job and livelihood.

At the time, my father was also a magistrate. In England, magistrates are highly distinguished members of the public who are nominated to be in the position of magistrates. These are volunteer positions that are filled by the public. A magistrate is very similar to a judge; they handle all the smaller issues of court and refer the larger criminal cases to a paid judge in what is called the Crown Court. My father served one day a week in court and specialized in family court. He would settle the cases of child support and child custody and sometimes have to make the painful decision to take children away from their parents in abusive situations. My father was in a position of extreme influence within the local courts of our city. When he found out that my friend's father, who just a few weeks earlier had tried to get him fired, was about to lose his license, my father acted. Most people would have let this man suffer the consequences. Many would have said it was the judgment of God. However, my father acted with grace and generosity. He knew he had the influence to help this man, and so he wrote a letter to the magistrate overseeing this man's case. My friend's father went to court and came out with a probationary warning, with his points sponged off the record.

I have never forgotten this story. In a season when I was questioning if the church even had a place in my life after experiencing all the hurt my family had been through the weeks prior, it was this incredibly generous act of grace that not only kept me in the faith but propelled me always to show grace and not revenge. This was a genuine act of generous influence.

You have influence. There are times when you could use that influence to crush others; that is the world's way. Christ's way is different! In the business environments you find yourself in, you may even get a pat on the back if you use your influence to crush others, but I would rather receive the blessings of God than a pat on the back from this world. Be generous with your influence, and watch as your influence grows.

PRAYER FOR GENEROSITY

Father, help me to live a life where my hands are open instead of my fists being shut tight. Grant me the grace to hold loosely to what I have in my possession and hold tightly to my belief in you. May I become generous with my time, giving to others when they need me. May I become generous with my resources, not holding onto them for my own pleasure but allowing them to be used for a greater purpose. May I become generous in my words, knowing the power they have. I desire to build people up, not tear them down. May I become generous with the influence you have given me, helping others walk through doors that otherwise they would not be able to. All I have is yours. I am not the owner, just the manager. Lord, give me the wisdom and the ability to manage well.

CHAPTER 12:
The Kingdom Builder Mentality

ONE OF MY FAVORITE PLACES TO VISIT IS THE BIBLE MUSEUM IN Washington, DC. Living so close to Washington, DC, we have the privilege of being able to visit it regularly. It is a great city full of beautiful buildings, incredible museums, and some great restaurants. However, the Bible Museum is my favorite. I would argue that it challenges any of the museums in the Smithsonian for its appearance and artifacts. The building is beautiful, and being a student and teacher of the Bible gives it the edge compared to the other attractions in DC.

When you walk into the building, towards the back on the ground floor, there are two walls full of bricks with names on them. To someone who lives in the world of Christian culture, some of the names on those bricks are familiar, and some are not. Some names are the owners of large corporations, some are the heads of very wealthy families, some are leaders of large international ministries or large churches, and some of the names are of individuals who decided to invest in helping to get the Bible Museum the funds they needed to transform an old warehouse in Washington DC into one of the best museums in the city. These names are the people who partnered with the organization to create what it is today. If your name is on a brick on a wall in a beautiful building, you know a large contribution has been made.

You may never get your name on a brick on a wall in a building here on Earth, but one day, I have a feeling you will see your name on a wall. The day you arrive in heaven, as you step through the pearly gates and walk the streets paved with Gold, you will see walls reaching up to the sky. I can imagine throughout the walls of heaven, we will see people's names. These are not the museum builders of this life, but they are the kingdom builders of eternity. As you marvel at the majesty and splendor of heaven, you notice a familiar name on the other side of the street at about eye level. As you cross the street, the name becomes clearer and bigger; it is your name. You found your name on the walls of heaven. However, your name is not written into a small clay or concrete brick. No, instead, your name is written into a large precious jewel, maybe a diamond, or jasper, a stone of sapphire, agate, maybe your name is written in a large emerald rock!

Suddenly, the memories of this life flood back, and the overwhelming sense of joy fills your thoughts. All that you did, those organizations you partnered with, those people you impacted, those projects you helped fund, those people you shared your story with, those nights of prayer, bringing your employees before God, those Bible verses you shared when others were in need, those meetings you decided to walk into being an ambassador for Christ, and the many other things you did on earth for God. It was worth it! Your name is etched into the walls of heaven, for you are a kingdom builder! This is a kingdom that knows no end, a kingdom that will reign for all of eternity. While the bricks and mortar of the Bible Museum will erode away, the names written into the walls of heaven will remain forever and forever. Congratulations, kingdom builder! You did it! You decided to forsake building your own kingdom while on earth and decided to be a part of building God's kingdom in heaven, and now look! Your name, written for eternity. All who pass by will know that you must have made a significant contribution to have your name written on the walls of heaven!

I do not know if any names will actually be written on the walls of heaven, but this is what I do know: If you decide to forsake building your own personal empire for the sake of helping to build the kingdom of God, then a great reward is awaiting you in heaven. A crown of glory is in your future. If you are wondering, the rewards of Earth pale in comparison to the rewards of heaven. For your business associates who are far away from God, this life is the only reward they get. The money, the cars, the houses, the vacations, the country club membership, the accolades, this is it; this is their heaven. For those who are far away from God, this is as good as it gets. You are different; the rewards of this earth are as bad as it gets. You have a greater reward awaiting you: a bigger house than all your friends, a mansion of no comparison in heaven! The work you do right here and now can either reward you with little on earth or can reward you with vast riches and joy in heaven; what will you choose?

The kingdom-builder mentality is heaven-focused, with eternity at the forefront of the mind. The kingdom builder is the one who understands ROI (Return on Investment) better than any hedge fund manager on Wall Street, for they understand that if I invest in heaven now, my return will be great!

> *Do not store up for yourselves treasures on earth, where moths and vermin destroy, and where thieves break in and steal. But store up for yourselves treasures in heaven, where moths and vermin do not destroy, and where thieves do not break in and steal. For where your treasure is, there your heart will be also.*
>
> — Matthew 6:19–21 (NIV)

These were the words of Jesus in His famous sermon on the Mount when He was teaching His followers the principles of the kingdom of heaven. Jesus encourages us to invest (store up) in heaven, to be a kingdom builder!

The book of James describes a grave end to those who ultimately invest in Earth and not heaven. It says,

> *Look here, you rich people. Weep and groan with anguish because of all the terrible troubles ahead of you. Your wealth is rotting away, and your fine clothes are moth-eaten rags. Your gold and silver are corroded. The very wealth you were counting on will eat away your flesh like fire. This corroded treasure you have hoarded will testify against you on the day of judgment.*
>
> — James 5:1–3 (NLT)

Then James continues,

> *"You have spent your years on Earth in Luxury, satisfying your every desire. You have fattened yourselves for the day of slaughter."*
>
> — James 5:5 (NLT)

These words are pretty strong! There is nothing wrong with wealth and good things. The blessings of God are bountiful. Money in itself is not bad; it is just a tool to be used, but when the love for money, wealth, and luxury starts to dictate your judgment and decisions, James tells us the end is not great! However, the Book of 1 Peter gives encouragement to those who decide to invest their wealth in heaven.

> *"We have a priceless inheritance, an inheritance that is kept in heaven for you, pure and undefiled, beyond the reach of change or decay."*
>
> — 1 Peter 1:4 (NLT)

We see a huge comparison between the riches of Earth and the riches of heaven. The riches of Earth are available now but do not last and build nothing. The riches of heaven are available later, but they last and help build a greater kingdom. So, where will you choose to invest?

As a business leader, you may be in a place financially where you have some bandwidth. What are you doing with the surplus of your resources? Are you pulling down barns to build bigger barns? Are you trusting the hedge fund managers of Wall Street to achieve a good ROI for you? Are you spending what you have on luxury, for you only live once? How are you managing the resources that you have at your disposal?

Let me challenge you and encourage you to be a kingdom builder. I believe God has not given you that business so you can have the financial freedom to not worry about finances. Yes, that is wonderful, but God gave you that business for a higher purpose, that is, to join with heaven to help build His kingdom! You are not blessed just so you can eat those blessings and squander them on luxury. You were blessed to be a blessing! When you bless others for the sake of Jesus, you are building His kingdom!

I heard it recently said when it comes to vision within the local church: "The pastor brings the vision, but it is the wealthy and business leaders who determine the pace at which the vision is fulfilled!" What this statement is saying is that the vision is great, but without the ability to fund the vision, it will not happen. God has given you the resources to help fund the vision for your local church! You may have much, or you may have little, but what you have is just enough in God's eyes, and He can use what you have in your hand to multiply that investment into a huge return in heaven.

I believe the local church in America and all across the world does not have a vision problem. I believe we have an acceleration problem! The quicker we can help accelerate the vision God has deposited into our churches, the quicker your friends and family are going to find Jesus, and ultimately, the quicker Jesus will come back, and you will get to see that incredible return on investment!

There are wells in Africa that need to be dug. There are children's homes in Asia that need to be built. There are women and children who need rescuing from human trafficking in Europe. There are Bible schools in Latin America that need to expand. There are intercity projects in the pipeline to help a generation with no hope that needs a financial boost. We have churches that need to be planted, missionaries that need to be sent, schools that need to be set up, houses of worship that need a new space, students who need to go to college, single mothers who need some breathing room, women's shelters that need to be raised up to provide a safe space, Bible translations that need to be written, radio programs that need to go out to unreached parts of the world, literature that needs to get to those in countries where the Gospel is banned, families who need to be fed, and homeless who need to find shelter. Ultimately, there is a generation of people on planet Earth, billions of people who are far away from God and will spend eternity in the screams and separation of hell if they do not hear the Gospel of Jesus Christ! We don't have a vision problem; we have an acceleration problem, and you can be part of the solution!

Are you a kingdom builder or an earth builder? Will your name be in lights in this life, or will your name be etched into the walls of heaven? Will you accept an ROI where moths eat and rust destroys, or will you receive an inheritance that is eternal?

You have the opportunity today to make a difference. God does not need your money. He has the riches of heaven at His disposal, but what He does need is your heart. Jesus said,

Where your treasure is, there the desires of your heart will be…No one can serve two masters. For you will hate one and love the other, you will be devoted to one and despise the other. You cannot serve God and be enslaved by money.

— Matthew 6:21–24 (NLT)

Where is your heart today? For where your treasure is, you will find your heart. God wants your heart, and for so many, it is money that has their heart. However, when you choose to have the mindset of a kingdom builder, money loses its grip. No longer does money have your heart; money becomes a tool and a resource to make a financial contribution to the retirement plan of heaven. What's more, God is in the matching business. When you invest in eternity, there is a supernatural multiplication that happens as well. God seems to take your small portion, and He turns it into more than you could ever imagine. Just like Jesus did with a young boy's lunch of two small fish and five small pieces of bread, which was turned into a feast for more than 20,000 people, He will take your small contribution and move heaven and earth with it.

That day, when you see your name on the walls of heaven, do not be surprised if a family from Africa comes up to you and says thank you for my fresh water. Do not be surprised if a child from Asia comes and says thank you for my home. Rejoice with the Pastor and the souls that are in heaven as you see the fruits of investing in that church plant or that Bible college in Latin America. Give that girl a hug who says thank you for helping to rescue me from the prostitution ring she had been trafficked into through Europe. Delight as you read the

Bible in the language you helped translate. Dance in the streets of gold with the ones who were hungry, thirsty, homeless, poor, and in bondage as your investment helped pave a way for a new life, a life full of hope and provision as they found life in Christ. Shout with joy as you pass all the people who would have never been able to join you on those streets in heaven had you not invested in your local church to make a difference and reach people far from God.

Your occupation is not the job title on your door! Your LinkedIn profile may say executive, accountant, lawyer, salesperson, educator, doctor, or contractor, but in the profile of heaven, it gives your real occupation: you are a *kingdom builder*.

PRAYER TO BE A KINGDOM BUILDER

Father, give me a vision of heaven. Paint the picture of the impact we are making in this life for the benefit of the next life. May I spend my days with the conviction and passion for helping build your kingdom and not my empire. May I be a vessel you can use to help prepare the way for people to find their way to heaven. Open up my heart so that I can be an answer to someone's prayer, not a hindrance to someone's faith. Oh God, I can not wait for the day I get to see what we are building here on Earth, finished on the streets of gold in heaven.

CHAPTER 13:

The Legacy Mentality

"**IT IS NOT ABOUT HOW YOU START THAT MATTERS. IT IS HOW YOU finish!**" This is a statement that leadership experts and speakers will tell their audience many times over throughout their careers. There is so much truth to that little statement; how you finish does matter. There is an issue that many do not talk about, though, that is, it is hard to finish well! Finishing well is hard because there are many different interpretations of what it means to finish well.

Does finishing well mean that when you are gone, people still respect you? Or do people say great things about you? Is finishing well staying out of trouble or controversy? Is it finishing what you intended to set out to do? Many would argue some or all of these points are what it means to finish well. However, I see an issue, especially for the Christ follower. This issue is that the majority of the examples the Bible provides us of people who finished well were often not respected by the world. There were many people who said not-so-good things about some of the heroes of faith. They were not far from their controversies, and some did not even finish what they started.

Take the patriarch of the faith, Abraham. While Abraham was full of faith, think about the fact that he took his wife's servant, impregnating her in order to try to create an heir to his family. Think about that for a moment. If that happened today, Abraham's reputation would be tarnished with scandal; we would not be saying he finished well.

Look at someone like Moses. He came onto the scene claiming that God had told him to lead the people of Israel out of Egypt into the promised land. Yet by the end of his life, the generation he had led had rebelled from God many times, grumbled daily, and all ultimately died in the wilderness, never reaching the promised land. Moses is a typical example of the world saying he started well but did not finish well.

David is another example: a man who was caught up in a scandal. His children were dysfunctional. He had one son that raped his daughter, and then another son killed that son. One son ran him out of Jerusalem and self-proclaimed himself as King before dying fighting his father's soldiers. Then, even at the end of his life, another son tried to force himself on the throne of Israel when David had chosen another son. David, throughout his life, had been caught up in a sexual scandal, murder, and the judgment that the killing by sword would never leave his house. David even presented a grand vision of building a temple for God, but that never happened in his life. There is no way, by today's standards, that David finished well!

We could go on and on about many of the heroes of faith and how they, on the surface, did not finish well. If we look at their mistakes and failings, then it is easy to point the finger and say that they started better than they finished. However, you can view these men through a different perspective, the legacy perspective, and see a quite different story. When it comes to a life of faith, whatever environment that life is played out in, it is not until you have left the room and given it time that you know how well you finished. Legacy cannot be judged from the events of your life or even in the immediate aftermath of your leaving. Legacy is judged by the next generation many years later.

Throughout the Old Testament, when people referred to God, they referred to Him as the God of Abraham. Despite all the faults Abraham had, the moments of weakness, and the unwise decisions he made, thousands of years later, when people thought about God, they linked God with the life of Abraham. This was a man who believed in a family as numerous as the stars in the sky, yet when he died, he only had one legitimate son, Isaac, and an illegitimate son, Ishmael. Yet, it was generations later when thousands upon thousands referred to their God as the God of Abraham.

Despite never achieving what he set out to do, Moses, dying with unfilled promises along with his peers, is now regarded as the greatest prophet of Israel, one of the greatest men ever to walk this planet.

David, leaving this life with his family in dysfunction, and his blueprints for the temple of God not even drawn, became the house of David, a dynasty that would know no end, sitting on the throne of Israel forever, ultimately setting up the way for Jesus.

There is a difference between trying to finish well and leaving a legacy. I do not encourage you to blow up your life and cause heartache and grief before you finish; that would just be going against everything we have discussed in the previous chapters. I would argue that finishing well is often measured by the standards of the world, but leaving a legacy can only be judged by time and God. I'm going to choose the legacy option every time. Let me explain.

Take a role at a company, for example. You know that you will not be in that role forever. Either you will leave that role for another one, you will be removed from that role, or you will be retired from that role. Every role you have started began with so much hope. You were happy to be in that role. The people you managed or the people who managed you had so much expectation that you probably started well. If you didn't start well, then it more than likely ended quickly. However, over time, change happened. It could have been a good change or bad change, but a change nonetheless. That role that seemed to mesh so well for you now started to have some frailties. You may have developed to now where that role was not satisfying, or the market may have changed, and you were not the right fit for that role anymore. There could have been some circumstances that happened or other opportunities that came along that forced you out of that role. Eventually, it was time to leave, and when you left, what was the reaction? We would all like to believe that a huge party was thrown in for us. That people wept as we walked out of the door; they celebrated what we had done, and our picture was kept on the wall to remind the whole company of our legendary status for years to come. The fond farewells, the gifts, the cards, admiration for what you had done. You get it; we all want to finish better than we started.

This is a wonderful thought, and it may happen for a few, but the reality is that for the majority of people, this is not their reality, especially for many leaders. Leaving is hard, and ending is not easy. Many times, people will question you, and some will think up a false reality of you as you leave. They will question your choices, your decisions, and the path you led. You will probably be the blame for that project or account that was not set up correctly. Your name will not be said in a friendly manner, and your picture, which is long gone, is in the trash.

Some of the best athletes of the past 100 years did not end well. Many of them were forced to retire due to injury; others kept playing until they were no longer significant. It is hard to finish well; that is why I believe we should focus on our legacy, not how strongly we finish. A life that finishes well can be celebrated, but a legacy can be built upon that lasts for generations. When you focus on legacy, the finishing well part takes care of itself.

When you leave a room, how do you leave it? Do you leave it better than how you came in? Did what you do while you were in the room help people make better decisions when you left the room? What is the trail that you leave behind wherever you go? Is that company or organization in a better place the day you leave compared to the day you arrived? Once again, these are all questions that can have subjective answers depending on who answers them, but those people who have a legacy mindset will always leave a room in a better place than where they found it, despite the opinions of what others may think.

The legacy mindset is a mentality that helps you build something so that others can build on top and make it better. It is creating a pathway so that the next generation can keep going and make it better.

While Abraham only had two sons, it was his own grandson who saw the incredible momentum build upon Abraham's promise. Abraham could have died with lost faith. He had not seen the promises of God, but instead of focusing on the failure of having two descendants, he passed this hope on to his son, who then passed it on to his son. When people refer to the one true God, they do not refer to God as the God of Abraham; they tag his son and grandson as well. He is known as the God of Abraham, Isaac, and Jacob. Now that is legacy!

Moses may have died in the wilderness with an unfulfilled promise, but he had raised up a leader in Joshua who would lead a generation who would conquer a land that Moses' generation only dreamt of. The moment that Moses was no more, Joshua rose to leadership and took Israel into the promised land and conquered the towns and peoples that Moses' generation was too frightened to confront. Joshua could not have done this unless Moses had paved the way; this is legacy.

David, when he was young, killed a giant named Goliath. Many years later, the Bible records that many of David's younger generals and mighty men are killing giants themselves or taking on great armies and winning. It could be argued that some of David's mighty men he trained and led did even greater things on the battlefield than David ever did. What's more, even though David did not build the temple of God, Solomon, his son, caught the vision and built a temple and a city in Jerusalem that was even more grand and splendid than David could ever have imagined. This is what legacy looks like.

Jesus, on the day He ascended into heaven, left a group of His followers shocked and troubled that He had left. Jesus had previously told His disciples that they would do greater things than even He did. How was this possible? With Jesus gone, all hope had gone? Yet just a few days later, the Holy Spirit was poured out upon these scared, confused disciples. The result was a city that found revival that spread to every corner of the globe! As believers, we are a result of the legacy Jesus left and the legacy the disciples left, and the next generation and the next and the next! We today are building upon what was built before us.

As a fifth-generation preacher, I am very aware that I am living in the favor and blessings of those who have gone before me. My grandfather's generation and those before him built a faith that lasted and transcended generation after generation. I am so thankful for parents who decided to build a legacy for their kids and grandkids instead of just trying to build their own kingdom. My father's greatest achievement in life was not found in any church he pastored or any large conference he spoke at. His greatest achievement was that he built a legacy of faith that his children and grandchildren are now building upon. This is legacy!

There is a verse in the Bible that haunts me. There are not many things in life I am fearful of, but there is a verse found in the book Judges that keeps me on my knees for the next generation and always gives me the motivation to build so that others can build on top.

> *"After that generation died, another generation grew up who did not acknowledge the Lord or remember the mighty things he had done for Israel."*
>
> — Judges 2:10 (NLT)

This is the generation that followed Joshua. Now, Joshua was a leader who fulfilled his purpose. He took over the mantel of leadership from Moses while the people of Israel were still in the wilderness. He rallied the people, got the priests together, and walked over a flooded Jordan River on dry ground as God stopped the river from flowing. He set up memorial stones to never forget what God had done. Under the leadership of Joshua, the people walked around the stronghold of Jericho and watched as God tore the walls down. They made inroads into the Promised Land of Cannan, enjoyed the prosperity of the land, and built towns and farms. They conquered mountains and dwelt in the plains as God gave them all they had believed since the days of Moses. Yet, despite all the miracles, all the fulfilled purpose, and all the prosperity, their kids walked away from God! While Joshua and his generation saw the power of God at work, they failed to build a legacy. There is no denying that Joshua finished well, but there was no legacy.

You may build the best business, innovate new things, provide the best life for your kids, provide greatly for your family, become famous in your industry, and receive accolades from your peers, but if you don't leave a legacy to build upon then what did you really build?

Your legacy does not start the day you die or retire. Your legacy starts today! You have the ability to leave a legacy that others can build upon as you leave that Monday morning meeting you attend each week. A legacy is not what you leave people when your final breath has been breathed; a legacy is what you leave behind wherever you go.

As an ambassador for Christ, when you took Jesus in the room with you, did He leave with you when you left, or did you leave a taste of Jesus for those who stayed in the room? When you left that organization, whatever they may have thought of you, did you leave them knowing there was something different, and that difference was Jesus? When you departed from that social event, did you depart with people desiring more of what the world can offer or with a desire for the joy that is deep down within you? When you leave, leave with people wanting more of Jesus, not more of you! When you leave, leave knowing that you have helped change the atmosphere and the landscape, and they cannot deny that Jesus was in the room. This is legacy!

A legacy mentality understands it is not about what I can build! It understands it is preparing the way for the next generation to build. Let us work hard to ensure that what they build will be built with eternity in mind, and they will be known as a generation of kingdom builders.

PRAYER FOR LEGACY

Father, may I be aware that what I do today will affect a generation coming behind me tomorrow. Help me to build, but build in a way that the next generation can build on top and build even better. Give me the wisdom to guide the next generation in your ways so they will rise up knowing you deeply. Help me to tell the stories of your faithfulness to the people I meet, my children, their friends, my grandchildren, and their friends, so they will always know there is a God who deeply loves them. God, let your presence not only be with me when I enter a room but let your presence continue to fill that room even long after I have left that room.

CHAPTER 14:
Conclusion

THE WHOLE PURPOSE OF THIS BOOK HAS BEEN TO HELP YOU UNDERstand that God's purpose for your life is greater than you possibly can understand. Your life matters, your business matters, and your mind matters. The principles of this book have been the ones that have changed the way I think. They took me from a conversation of feeling stuck on a hot July afternoon to a place of freedom, provision, and greater purpose than I had ever felt before. These are principles that I have applied not just to my business life but to every facet of my being, principles that have left many of the people in my world scratching their heads because I have decided that my life is going to be different from the world.

Many of the world's principles are sound, solid ways to achieve much, but for the Christ follower, there has to be a difference within you. You are a citizen of heaven, and the principles of heaven do not always make sense to those who think with an earthly mentality.

We started off with the Bible scripture from Romans 12:

> *Therefore, I urge you, brothers and sisters, in view of God's mercy, to offer your bodies as a living sacrifice, holy and pleasing to God—this is your true and proper worship. Do not conform to the pattern of this*

world, but be transformed by the renewing of your mind. Then you will be able to test and approve what God's will is—his good, pleasing, and perfect will.

— Romans 12:1–2 (NIV)

There is a world that is seeking to shape your mind and your will. It markets itself well, working hard to tell you that you are the center of the universe, that all that matters is you, you can be whoever you want to be, and do not let anything stop you. It sounds good, right? But, it is soul-destroying. Seeking a life outside the purposes of God is an uphill task that will never be fulfilled. It is like using a baseball bat to play golf. Yes, you can advance the ball forward, but it is going to be a long and painful journey; you will never find the end goal. For the end goal is eternity, and without God, your eternity is doomed; with God, your eternity is full of hope and joy.

I pray and hope that the principles in this book have helped you think differently about the marketplace and your role in it every day. If you can think about your impact in terms of heaven a little more throughout a workday and with the people you interact with, then the goal of this book has been achieved. However, I know that the more you allow the Holy Spirit to transform your mind away from the patterns of this world and towards the purposes of Jesus, the more you will find the abundance, blessings, favor, and fulfillment that comes with the territory.

Throughout this book, I have intentionally avoided giving tips and ways to lead and conduct yourself in the marketplace. The reason for this is that while nuggets of wisdom and tips from experts have great value, seeking the Holy Spirit, allowing

God to transform your mind, and understanding your identity and purpose in the marketplace are more important than any tip one can give. As you walk into meetings, take phone calls, manage your team, present your product to clients, network at the industry conference, or have lunch with a co-worker, having the mind and leading of the Holy Spirit is the most valuable asset you can access. Without the Holy Spirit, we are left with the wisdom of man. I am not knocking the advice of wise people, but give me the Holy Spirit any day.

I remember reading an article in Forbes magazine several years ago entitled "Why Humble Leaders Make the Best Leaders."[6] Humility is often quite misunderstood. We do not think of the best leaders as humble. We think of them as strong and decisive, making the hard decisions and not backing down. Yet, when you study what separates the best CEOs from everyone else, it is humility that comes to the top. Many people think that humility is thinking less of yourself. However, humility is quite the opposite. Thinking less of yourself is self-deprivation, and good leaders do not self-deprive, especially those who have been transformed by the power and grace of Jesus Christ. For the Christ follower is confident in who they are; they are a child of God, a joint heir with Christ; we are not just anyone. We are the ambassadors of the Most High King, favored with the power of heaven backing us up. We are kingdom builders who one day will find their name on the walls of heaven. We have been adopted into the family of God, and there should be no talk of self-deprivation.

---

[6] Hyman, J. (2018) "Why Humble Leaders Make the Best Leaders," Forbes. Available at: https://www.forbes.com/sites/jeffhyman/2018/10/31/humility/?sh=527b9c9b1c80 (Accessed: 26 September 2023).

Humility is different. It is not thinking less of yourself; it is thinking about yourself less. This is what separates the best leaders from everyone else. If you can separate your own feelings, needs, and desires for the sake of the purpose and mission before you, then you are well on your way to achieving success. For the Christ follower who is navigating the corporate jungle or living in the marketplace, you have a purpose and mission that is before you. It is the mission of heaven to take the Gospel of Jesus to the nations: to share the love, grace, and mercy of Christ with those near us. It is to change the atmosphere and the environments we find ourselves in so the Holy Spirit can do the work that only the Holy Spirit can do. It is to build not an earthly empire but to join with heaven and build the kingdom of heaven. It is to leave a legacy so that those coming behind us can build and not forget.

If you allow your mind to be renewed and transformed by the spirit of God, you will not only be able to navigate the corporate or business jungle you find yourself in; no, through the help and power of the Holy Spirit, you will start to see your environment turn from an unstable jungle to a beautiful garden where Jesus is moving and working.

Will you offer up your life as a living sacrifice to God? Not copying the customs or patterns of this world, but instead, will you let God transform your life by changing your mindset? If you do, the promises of God, which are sure and true, tell us that you will find God's will for your life, a purpose for you that is pleasing, full of joy, and perfect for who God created you to be.

You are in those environments for a reason. There is purpose for you in the marketplace. Go knowing it is not because of you but all because of Christ. You are an ambassador of the King, with a sling in your hand, the favor of God on you, aligned with your life in the right order, knowing that abundance is all around, with God giving His manna for today. That there are divine appointments God has set up for today and the future. He is leading you today to bless others with the blessings you have been given and to help build the kingdom of God, leaving a legacy for the generation behind to build upon.

You have got this! You are making a difference! Go be all God has created you to be!

ABOUT THE AUTHOR

ALEX IS A PASTOR, KEYNOTE SPEAKER, TOP SALES EXECUTIVE, AND entrepreneur. Through his work within the local church, he is helping to cultivate a culture where marketplace leaders experience the value of being able to help set the pace for the fulfillment of the vision of the local church. He lives in Forest Hill, Maryland, with his wife and son, where he serves as kingdom-builder pastor at Freedom Church, Bel Air, MD, and a risk advisor at the Leavitt Group.